Open Your Heart

The 7 secrets of intimate relationships

Sue Plumtree

This edition first published in the UK 2017 by Life Long Books, Richmond, Surrey, UK

Design and typography by Tim Gray

ISBN: 978-0-9560270-1-6

Text © Sue Plumtree

Sue Plumtree has asserted her right under the Copyright, Designs and Patents Act 1988 to be identified as the author of this work.

All rights reserved

No part of this book may be reproduced or utilized in any form or by any means, electronic or mechanical, without prior permission in writing from the copyright owner.

Contact details:
www.sueplumtree.com
sue@sueplumtree.com
Mobile 07903 795027

Also by Sue Plumtree:

Dancing With The Mask: Learning To Love And Be Loved

*To my Lolly,
who showed me what love truly is.*

Contents

Foreword 1 by Carleen Glasser	1
Foreword 2 by Nick Williams	4
Readers' comments	7
About the author	9
Autobiography in five chapters	10
Introduction	12
Chapter 1 – From pain to fulfilment	16
Chapter 2 – Why happy relationships are so important	27
Chapter 3 – How limiting beliefs destroyed my relationships	35
Chapter 4 – How my system was born	42
Chapter 5 – Getting started: keep a journal	54
Chapter 6 – Begin your journey	57
Chapter 7 – Life Principles – The Authentic Self-Exploration Roadmap	60
Chapter 8 – The Reflect and Restore Regimen	89

Chapter 9 – Emotional communication – The Emotional Revitaliser System	123
Chapter 10 – The Passion and Intimacy Generator	140
In conclusion	157
Last words …	158
Special offer	159
Acknowledgements	160

Foreword 1
by Carleen Glasser

Carleen Glasser, MA, CT/RTC, is CEO of William Glasser, Inc., and Senior Instructor and Relationship Coach for the William Glasser Institute International Inc.

When we are very young, we frequently find passionate love but, much to our dismay, the feeling is soon lost. The irony is we have absolutely no idea why this happens.

I came across *Reality Therapy* by Dr. William Glasser while I was still married.

His ideas and his clear and understandable solutions to some of life's most challenging problems around relationships changed my life, and I decided to learn as much as I could about them.

The one idea that made the biggest impact on me was about taking charge of my own life, and I decided to do just that. That's when I started my training in Reality Therapy (now known as The William Glasser Institute) and became certified in 1986.

Then in 1993, a full ten years after I first read *Reality Therapy*, my ailing marriage of many years eventually came to an end.

After Bill (Glasser) was widowed and some time after my divorce, I finally met the man I had admired for so many years. Over time we became close and married 5 years later.

It was with him that I first understood what love really means.

In him I found that singular connection none of us can live without, that one essential friend to love and be loved by.

I tell my story to illustrate how ideas like those in Sue Plumtree's book, *Open Your Heart: the 7 Secrets of Strong and Loving Relationships* can be seen played out in real lives. Ideas like her Seven Secrets were actualized in my own experience and I am grateful she has revealed them here to the world.

Sadly, so many relationships fail and so few of the people in them have any clue why they fail over and over again. What is worse, they also have no clue what they could do about it.

This mystery can be solved with insights such as the ones provided in Open Your Heart: The 7 Secrets of Strong and Loving Relationships.

My late husband, the world renowned psychiatrist William Glasser, M.D., would have applauded the work Sue Plumtree has done to contribute to the knowledge people must have to finally succeed in their relationships.

Her words speak volumes in this book and I encourage you and your partner to read it together. By doing so, you will enjoy one of the most rewarding journeys of your lives.

This well-spent time discovering how to improve your relationship could make all the difference in the world to you and your partner struggling with the mystery of finding true and lasting happiness with each other.

Foreword 2 by Nick Williams

Nick Williams is a best-selling author and inspirational speaker, based in London.

One of the great adventures of my younger life was my "search for love." I became a seeker and did extensive research. Some of the time it was fun, but only for a while.

It was a strategy that was doomed to failure and disappointment.

However much I sought love, I didn't seem to find what I thought I was looking for. But the search eventually led me to a realization that would change the trajectory of my life.

What I came to realise was that I sought love from others because I didn't really feel I was that loveable. I was looking for someone else to love me more than I actually loved myself, a woman to prove to me that I wasn't as unlovable as I feared I was. I was looking for someone to rescue me from how unkind and unloving I was being to myself.

Ouch! Good luck with that one!

And, even when I did find someone who loved me, I didn't feel worthy of it and somehow messed things up, sabotaged it or blew it. Secretly, I was demanding love whilst at the same time feeling unworthy of it when it arrived.

I finally chose to start a journey to learn to love myself, to accept myself and to see the good in me that I was desperately hoping that others might see in me. I started looking for the love 'in here' rather than the love 'out there.'

I am now more able to love out of generosity rather than need.

Over the 21 years of my relationship with my partner Helen I have learned how much my self-love has made me more lovable and how, unexpectedly, it grew Helen's love for me.

It would have been wonderful if Sue had written her book, *'Open Your Heart: The 7 Secrets of a Strong and Loving Relationship'* to guide me all those years ago.

Sue is one of those generous souls who has been on her own journey of remembering the truth of love. She has done her personal extensive research and has lived to tell the tale. She has allowed herself to be broken open and opened up again and again, so that she can finally experience true love.

Sue is one of those wonderful souls who has pioneered and led the way. She is generous enough to turn her learning into a gift for all of us. Sue has transformed the pain and challenges of her life into gold in her book *'Open Your Heart: The 7 Secrets of a Strong and Loving Relationship'* that we can all benefit from.

I have known Sue personally for a number of years through the Inspired Entrepreneur community that I used to run in

London. I have seen her joys and struggles, I have seen her lift herself up over and over again, and now that she is standing on higher ground, she shares the view with us all.

Thank you Sue for the journey you have been on and sharing yourself through writing '*Open Your Heart: The 7 Secrets of a Strong and Loving Relationship*' which is such a hopeful and practical book.

And thank you, Sue, for being you.

Read this book and open your heart to greater love, for yourself and everyone in your life

Readers' comments

"What I love about Sue's book is how she gets straight to the point without loads of theory, in a gentle and easy to understand way. Her tools are practical and insightful. I love the way she takes us on a journey with her: how it was for her, how she learned, the mistakes she made along the way and where she is now. It makes me feel that she cares about me, understands where I am at and has the knowledge, wisdom and patience to support me in my own journey." *Riana Avis*

"I found your book very truthful and honest, that it came from the heart." *Bernie Gage*

"I found I didn't want to put the book down! I loved the fact that YOU are in the book and that YOU are just like me!" *Joan Mercer*

"This book gives you a safe place to 'find' and 'hold' yourself while you explore the real meaning of being in a relationship - how we attract and impact upon our chosen relationship. Learn how to truly love and be loved in return." *Mona De Silva*

"I wish I'd had the privilege of reading this book all those years ago. If I had then maybe I would have avoided a costly divorce after 42 years of marriage and I would still be a married man. Initial problems in any marriage can be reconciled if the couple both have access to this book." *Ajayi Oguntokun*

"I felt connected and hooked to your story and your teachings from the moment I started reading. The tone is very wise, warm and loving." *Marva Johnson-Jones*

About the author

Sue Plumtree is The Over 50s Love Specialist – coach, writer and speaker. Her passion is to enable people to build strong and loving relationships.

Her knowledge and wisdom are not only based on her formal training as a coach but on her own experience of having gone through the pain of an unhappy 37 year marriage which she finally left, aged 60.

Over the 12 years that followed, Sue went on to build a remarkable life – she wrote her second book and autobiography, 'Dancing With The Mask: Learning To Love And Be Loved' because she wanted people to know that they didn't have to stay in a painful situation; that they were not as helpless as they often believe themselves to be.

She developed loving and supportive friendships, built a hugely successful coaching practice working with women over 50 and, in December 2015 aged 70, met Paul, her friend, her lover and soulmate.

Sue has learned the hard way what does not work in relationships and she knows now what it takes to build a relationship that is strong, loving and intimate.

She typically works with women over 50 on a one-to-one basis on her 6-month programme, 'Live Your Best Years Yet'.

Autobiography in five chapters

I walk down the street.
There is a deep hole in the pavement.
I fall in.
I am lost......I am hopeless.
It isn't my fault.
It takes forever to find a way out.

I walk down the same street.
There's a deep hole in the pavement.
I pretend I don't see it.
I fall in again.
I can't believe I'm in the same place.
It isn't my fault.
It still takes a long time to get out.

I walk down the same street.
There's a deep hole in the pavement.
I see it is there.
I still fall in… it's a habit.
My eyes are open.
I know where I am.
It is my fault.
I get out immediately.

I walk down the same street.
There's a deep hole in the pavement.
I walk around it.

I walk down another street.

Nyoshui Khenpo

Introduction

*"All truths are easy to understand once they are
discovered; the point is to discover them."*
Galileo Galilei

This book is based on eight fundamental truths.

Truth No. 1

When you figure out exactly how you jointly created your disappointing relationships, you will be less likely to repeat your mistakes.

Whether you know it or not, you and anybody you have a relationship with have jointly created that relationship, whether fulfilling or disappointing. However, even though you had no idea you were doing it, the results were often not only unwanted but also seemed random and unpredictable.

With this new knowledge you will be able to develop new strategies that will enable you to revitalise your relationships.

Truth No. 2

Your relationship with yourself shapes your relationships with everybody else.

That's because people take you at your own valuation. It also explains why, getting to know, love, respect and trust yourself, is absolutely fundamental. When you do, you will make different choices that will bring you better results.

Truth No. 3

Your thoughts affect your feelings and your feelings determine everything you say and do.

While your actions, including your words, create your reality, the process starts with your mindset, that is, with your thoughts, with what you tell yourself about yourself and others. This is what determines the quality of your life, your relationships and even the state of your health and wellbeing.

Truth No. 4

You cannot force another person to change.

They will only do so if they're willing and able to change. The only person you can change is yourself. So stop blaming others for whatever makes you feel miserable, helpless and hopeless, and take responsibility for your own happiness.

Truth No. 5

When you're clear about your personal boundaries, you will be in a good position to change another person's behaviour towards you.

But first you will need to be clear about how you do NOT want to be treated and how you prefer to be treated instead. That will form the basis of your personal boundaries. Only when you're clear about them will you be able to take the steps you need to take to change the way other people engage with you.

Truth No. 6

To change your relationships you need to take the initiative.

You need to connect with people in a different way. This will enable your partner and others to hear you without becoming defensive.

Truth No. 7

Doing things that you enjoy is essential to your happiness, health and wellbeing.

This keeps your emotional engine topped up. When it is, you will feel good about yourself and be better equipped to continue to give.

Truth No. 8

When it comes to implementing changes, you need to take baby steps.

Not only do they feel less scary and more do-able, they often produce results that are out of all proportion to the size of the action taken.

If any of these truths have chimed with you, please read this book and I will show you how to build successful relationships that are solid and enduring.

In the coming chapters I will share with you how you can move from feeling unloved and unappreciated to feeling cherished, valued and supported so you can build the life and relationships you truly deserve.

Sue Plumtree
The Over 50s Love Specialist

Chapter 1 – From pain to fulfilment

> *"And then, you just realise that everything you've ever needed to succeed lies inside of you. You just really needed to look within and draw from the strength that lies there. Nothing is impossible at that very moment."*
> *Ufuoma Apoki, writer*

I woke up one morning noticing, as I had more and more often lately, the tight knot in my stomach and a sense of unshed tears.

I tried to think of a time when I hadn't felt like that but couldn't. It was as if I had been feeling like this forever.

I looked at Jim, my husband, who lay sleeping beside me, snoring gently, and I felt nothing.

I had to get ready for work but I paused, trying to collect my thoughts, trying to work out why I felt like this, even after more than 30 years.

All I ever wanted was to be loved or, to put it more accurately, all I ever wanted was to *feel* loved.

Instead, all I'm feeling is lonely, empty and disconnected.

Yes, lonely, most of all. I wonder, when did it all start?

My first collision with reality in my marriage

If you'd been with me that evening in June 1966, you'd find me standing by the little kitchen table.

It's a cosy little kitchen. I can smell the spicy aroma of the dish I'm preparing. I can hear the tick-tock of the clock on the wall. And there's a gas meter on the wall that I have to remember to keep topped up with half-crown coins, especially when I'm preparing dinner.

I've only been in this little flat 3 months so it still feels new.

It's almost 6:00 o'clock in the evening and he's due home from work any minute now.

I'm feeling really nervous because I've done something I've never done before, and I've been wondering how he would react. Will he smile? Will he feel moved? Will he take me into his arms and whisper tenderly how lucky he is to have found me…?

Oh, my goodness! There he is. Right on time. Jim, my husband of 3 months steps into the kitchen.

When I look at him he still reminds me of a young Cary Grant. He's got the cutest dimples! I think I first fell in love with his dimples!

He gives me a peck on the cheek. I wait for him to say something but he doesn't.

In the end, I can't contain myself any longer and I burst out, "Well? Did you see it?"

He turns to me and says with a cold tone of voice, "If you're referring to that silly little note, then, yes, I did. Don't do that again. It doesn't do anything for me."

My heart stops. How can he say that? I wrote him a love note and he tells me it doesn't do anything for him!

I burst into tears and run out of the kitchen into the bathroom, and I sob and sob and sob until I'm spent.

I splash cold water on my face. My eyes are red and puffy, my face, all blotchy.

I look at my image in the mirror and it looks back at me, clearly despising my over-reaction.

"You pathetic woman! Look at you!"

I can't help replying:

"But, I thought that, if I could make him fall in love with me I would know I was loveable, that I was attractive, but now…" My voice trails into silence and hopelessness.

The story of the baby elephant

The next years remind me of the story of the baby elephant.

A circus bought a baby elephant and to keep it safe, they chained it onto a stake so it couldn't wander off and be trampled by the other bigger beasts.

Inevitably, the baby elephant grew to become a BIG elephant and, of course, they removed the chain. The elephant could go anywhere he wanted – but, instead, he kept going round and round that little space around the stake which was all he'd known for so long.

And that's exactly what I do too.

For the next many years, I go into total denial.

But my body doesn't let me get away with it.

Things go from bad to worse.

It's decision time

Today it's June 2002 and I'm about to meet my friend, Ilana, for coffee which is something we do regularly.

Ilana is a Russian woman in her thirties, about an inch or so shorter than I, blonde, beautifully dressed, very chic. She limps because she had polio as a child.

We meet at a café off Regent Street in London. It has an old-fashioned décor, a huge mirror at the back of the room and plush chairs with red upholstery. The surface of the tables are covered with landscapes of forests and mountains and lakes. We love coming here because it's so relaxing.

Today, Ilana is already there and she's sitting at a table in the middle of the room. As I enter the café she watches me with a look of horror in her face and exclaims,

"Sue! You look awful! What on earth are you doing on those crutches?"

I sit down heavily and everything bursts out of me – everything I held back over so many years.

"Ilana, I can't tell you how awful things are. A few years ago, years before you and I even met, I developed bulimia. I really believe that the only reason I'm sitting here today is that I didn't want to die! And then there were those depression episodes for which my GP prescribed Valium. It's a miracle I didn't get addicted!

And now, over the last few years, I've been experiencing severe pains. This time it's my knee. The pain is just awful. I can't get around without these crutches!

Ilana, I'm so scared of becoming disabled, helpless, dependent but, every time I try to tell Jim how I feel, he just says "Don't be silly!"

"I feel so alone, Ilana. I feel dismissed, unimportant, unloved!"

Open Your Heart

Ilana says, "Oh darling, I knew things were bad but I had no idea they were this bad!"

"It's just that things have got even worse, Ilana. I've reached a point where I don't even feel like an attractive woman anymore! My confidence has hit rock bottom and I don't know what to do. I can't talk to him. When I try, he doesn't even bother to reply! I know it sounds awful but I don't know if he even likes me!"

Ilana asks, "What are you going to do?"

"Ilana, I've been thinking about this for a very long time and I have come to realise that I can't do this anymore! I've had enough! I've decided to leave him."

I discover it's easier said than done

The minute I decide to leave, my Gremlin, my negative inner critic, goes on the attack:

"What do you mean you want to be happy? What do you mean you deserve better and you want to leave? You're 59, for goodness sake!"

"What makes you think you could survive on your own? You have never lived alone! You know you depend on Jim to change the lightbulbs and fuses! You'd never be able to cope!"

"How can you possibly leave poor Jim? He's 69! How can you abandon him now that he's old? What kind of cruelty is that? What kind of selfishness? Is that what I taught you?!" – that's my mum 's voice.

My Gremlin keeps hammering away at me until I feel so scared, so overwhelmed with self-doubt that I slink back into that little room, my comfort zone, where I tell myself it's safe and familiar and not as bad as I make it out to be.

I tell myself staying with Jim is the sensible thing to do. Doing anything else would be far too risky, too unrealistic. It would be irresponsible for me to even consider it.

I dig deep into myself and find my courage

I stay in my comfort zone until finally, in spite of the Gremlin, I come to see that the pain of staying in a relationship where I feel unloved, dismissed, rejected, unimportant, even unattractive as a woman, is worse than the fear of the unknown.

It's March 2004 when I finally walk out. I'm nearly 60.

There's light at the end of the tunnel – and that light is dazzling.

In the 12 years that follow, I discover I'm more capable, more resilient, more resourceful than I could have ever imagined.

I start making good choices – choices that work for me.

Today, at 72 I have none of the conditions associated with older people.

I feel better than ever before. My energy levels are high. I haven't caught a bad cold in years and, when I get a sniffle, it only lasts a few days.

I no longer pretend I have got it all figured out and decide to start allowing myself to be emotionally vulnerable. In other words, I am prepared to show I don't know it all and ask for help from friends or professionals.

That's scary because I always believed I needed to present myself as strong and independent – otherwise people would think I was needy and demanding and that frightened the hell out of me.

What I'm actually discovering, to my utmost amazement, is that what I'd been doing all those years was keeping love at arm's length, quite the opposite of what I yearned for.

Now I'm beginning to attract the most wonderful friendships - people who are generous, open-hearted and supportive. And, for the first time in my life, I feel truly loved.

I am building a new life for myself:

I have become a certified life coach and now I'm developing a life-coaching practice. I discover I'm good at it.

I've written two books. My second is my autobiography. I wanted people to know that life doesn't have to stay painful –

that there IS another way to live. I discover I have a message to share and I've found my voice.

I have even started going on little adventures. My most recent one was in November 2015 when I went to Turkey on a paragliding holiday! What an experience that was! Absolutely awesome! And I was 70 at the time...

Surely life can't get any better? But it does.

Just a couple of weeks after returning from Turkey I meet a man – a man who turns out to be the man of my dreams, the love of my life, my lover, my friend, my soul mate – my partner.

And the cycle of my life is complete – from the young girl who yearned to be loved, to the young woman who made many mistakes in her quest for love to the mature woman who found more than she ever dreamed of finding.

I discover why I'm here

I've started running workshops about transforming relationships. I'm being invited to speak about love and relationships, primarily our love for ourselves and how it shapes all our other relationships. I speak about the connection between the quality of our relationships and our physical, emotional and mental health and wellbeing.

This is what I'm discovering.

There are thousands of people who, just as I was for such a long time, are in an unhappy relationship, feeling taken for granted, rejected, dismissed.

They stay because:

- they don't believe they deserve to be loved, to be cherished, to be valued and appreciated
- they're afraid they won't be able to cope on their own
- they feel more comfortable staying with what they feel is familiar and safe without realising that, while it may be familiar, it's definitely not safe.

I know what the pain of feeling unloved is like. I know what the pain of feeling unimportant is like. I know what it's like to be taken for granted.

And I also know the joy that comes from being able to love whole-heartedly and being truly loved in return.

And, most important of all, I know what works and what doesn't work in a relationship.

And I finally know why I'm here.

Now it's YOUR turn.

Looking back at your experience, you will use what did NOT work in your relationship and build something new, something different, something better.

You have more power than you can possibly imagine; you have more wisdom than you believe possible – these are your resources. And, in this book, you will discover more.

This is YOUR time!

Chapter 2 – Why happy relationships are so important

*"Resentments are like taking poison and
expecting the other person to die."*
Anon

First, let me tell you something you may find hard to believe:

You are lovable. You are unique. You deserve to be loved, valued, appreciated. You deserve to be heard and, most of all, you deserve to be treated with consideration, with decency and, yes, with respect.

And that's irrespective of how long you've been in your relationship.

I know this is not how things often are but that doesn't make it any less true.

In this book I will show you how to build the kind of relationships that honours who you are.

As I have already said above, I know what works and what doesn't work in relationships.

I also know that you already have all the wisdom and resources you need to build happy relationships. The problem is that they have been covered up with so many 'limiting beliefs', that you've lost touch with them.

Part of the purpose of this book is to enable you to remove those 'limiting beliefs' until you are in touch with who you really are.

When you reach that stage you will realise that it's time to reclaim your life and take charge of your own happiness.

For many of us, happiness includes a loving and intimate relationship. But a loving and intimate relationship isn't essential for our happiness.

Some of us prefer close companionship, kinship, a feeling of connection with another human being.

Why are good relationships so important?

Far too many people are living lives that don't really fit them anymore, lives they have actually outgrown. Are you one of them? Are you wasting your emotional energy on something which is just not working for you and could even be making you feel worthless, unwell and unable to fulfil your true potential?

Here are a couple of examples of what's possible.

- Based on my guiding principles, you manage to revitalise your own existing relationship, moving from one that was unfulfilling to a new model that is strong, loving and supportive – but see the caution below.

- You're not currently in a relationship and are looking for the right partner. Once you have found them, you then manage to build something special, particularly when either one of you had an unhappy relationship in the past. You are able to use your past experience in a positive way and can guide your new partner to do the same.

First, some words of caution.

Here's something important you need to know.

To transform an unhappy relationship into one that is more fulfilling, you need to take the initiative and be pro-active. Learn as much as you can about how good relationships work. Carry out your own research, read books about relationships or perhaps discuss things with trusted friends or an outside advisor.

Most importantly, get to know yourself first, your real needs and wants, what truly matters to you, what you need to be happy in your relationship – all things you will discover by reading this book.

Relationships – positive or negative – are, of course, created by the two people involved.

If, despite all your efforts, your partner doesn't respond, you will then be in a much stronger position to make a new choice whatever that choice may be. And, having done your research and homework, your choice will suit the person you really are.

That being said, I would always encourage you to do the best you can to revitalise your current relationship if there's still some affection.

The costs of unhappy relationships

Emotional

There have been many studies carried out by researchers and professors which have been published in a variety of medical journals, including the American Medical Association and others.

Their findings show the high emotional cost of staying in an unsatisfactory relationship where you feel unhappy, discouraged, frustrated.

You probably feel taken for granted and that causes resentment. You might even feel, or have been made to feel through your partner's behaviour, unworthy of being loved – all of which damages your sense of self-worth, self-confidence and self-belief.

As your relationship deteriorates, it's not only you who suffers. Your children, the rest of your family and, yes, your partner too – you all suffer. Even your friendships may become strained.

As for the reaction of children, the family law organisation Resolution has found that most young people who have experienced divorce do not believe parents should stay together for the sake of the children.

And Scientific American has found that, although divorce affects most children in the short run, research suggests that they recover rapidly after the initial blow.

In a study carried out by psychologist E. Mavis Hetherington of the University of Virginia and her then graduate student Anne Mitchell Elmore, they found that, while many children experience short-term negative effects from divorce, especially anxiety, anger, shock and disbelief, these reactions typically diminish or disappear by the end of the second year.

Health and Wellbeing

Studies published in 2014 in the Journal of Health and Social Behaviour found that couples in marriages riddled with rows and criticism experience increased risk of heart disease and that the effect was greater than the protective effect from 'good' marriages.

The researchers used data from 1,198 married people who were part of the National Social Life, Health and Aging Project in America.

They found that the tense environment, where there's a constant sense of resentment, argumentativeness and criticism, can produce excessive levels of cortisone that cause both physical and mental health problems. These may include weight-gain due to comfort eating, high blood-pressure and other related conditions that could lead to strokes.

A less severe consequence but nonetheless debilitating, is a lowered immunity resulting in a variety of infections, more headaches and colds which take longer to get rid of. You may also experience anxiety, depression, irritability and/or high stress levels.

Financial

As we all know too well, relationship break-up has significant financial costs, including solicitors' expenses, moving house and starting up all over again, all of which can considerably affect the quality of the next stage of your life.

Even so, if you're willing to make adjustments, you can make it work.

My feeling is that the cost of staying in an unsatisfactory long-term relationship which makes you feel rejected, dismissed or unimportant is far higher and more damaging than that of any life-changing adjustments you may need to make to create your own better future.

Social

If you decide to leave your marriage you may find that the loyalty of joint friends is torn. These friends may feel they have to take sides or withdraw altogether, as happened to me.

The result can be, at least temporarily, sadness, social isolation and loneliness.

However, you will significantly ease this situation if you begin to widen your social circle long before you actually implement your decision to make fundamental changes in your life.

Conclusion

Leaving the relationship is, of course, an option and sometimes even a very positive one.

But, if you don't know what went wrong, there's a very real danger of recreating the same problem all over again in your next relationship.

So here's a question.

If you're currently in an unhappy relationship where you've forgotten what it feels like to be loved and where you would like to rekindle the romance you once had and build something *different*, where you feel special, cherished and appreciated, doesn't it make sense that you need to not only change what you're doing now, but also try to understand exactly what that 'different' is? You need to have a vision of your future.

Or, if you're currently single and have been in unhappy relationships in the past, doesn't it make sense that you learn how to build relationships that are loving, solid and durable?

Chapter 3 – How limiting beliefs destroyed my relationships

> *"You have the power in the present moment to change limiting beliefs and consciously plants seeds for the future of your choosing. As you change your mind, you change your experience."*
> Serge King, Ph.D., writer

It's March 2004 and I have just got back from a three-day course called 'Spiritual Renewal', led by Miranda Holden, a spiritual counsellor.

I'm still in a state of shock.

One of the things Miranda did was to lead us through a forgiveness meditation. She first took us through a relaxation routine, then she asked us:

"Whom do you want to forgive?"

I'd been reading books on forgiveness and going through the various exercises that would enable me to forgive Jim for everything he said or didn't say, and everything he did or didn't do that made me feel so unhappy and brought us to this place, about to part ways. None of the exercises had worked.

But here I was, getting ready to experience this forgiveness meditation. I was sceptical, unconvinced it would work but willing to give it a go.

Miranda asked us again, "Whom do you want to forgive?"

I couldn't believe it when, instead of saying "Jim", what came out of my mouth was, "Me".

That surprised me, but worse was to come:

"And what part of you do you want to forgive?", Miranda continued.

And this is what I blurted out:

"I want to forgive the part of me that believed I wasn't worth loving."

I couldn't believe what had come out of my own mouth. I was devastated.

I'd had no idea that this was what I believed but when I looked at my relationships – from my marriage to every single one of my friendships – I saw, to my distress, that it was true. I really did believe I wasn't worth loving.

That realisation marked the moment when everything changed.

What it takes to be happy

One of the most important things I have learnt is that happiness is not a destination, but a choice that flows from your mindset.

I explain in more detail what mindset is in Chapter 7 – 'Life Principles' but, briefly, mindset is a person's attitudes, values and beliefs that causes them to have certain thoughts and opinions. They predetermine a person's reactions, responses, and how they interpret everything that happens to them.

Research shows that, to feel happy, you need a balance between

- meaningful work (paid or unpaid)
- family and close friends
- a close and intimate relationship which may be sexual or non-sexual
- good health and a sense of well-being,
- spirituality
- fun
- sufficient money so you don't have to worry from one day to the next.

The combination of the above makes you feel good about yourself. When you feel good about yourself, everything about you – your body language and your general behaviour – become attractive to others in all sorts of ways.

But back to real life. We don't all have a loving family or possibly even a family at all, fun can be a bit difficult when you have to deal with life's challenges, including a low sense of well-being and poor health, not everybody is physically able to get out and about, and lack of money can be a problem.

All of this is true – BUT that does not make the original premise false. This is what's true:

It doesn't matter what happens to us – what matters is how we react and respond to life events and circumstances.

So, given the above, let's take each of these depressing points one at a time.

Loneliness is, as I know all too well, a very painful experience. And it's even worse when you feel lonely within your marriage or when you're with friends.

But think: you're not the only one who feels lonely and isolated. The underlying message in this book is that, if you want to change anything, you're the one who needs to take that first step. I won't deny it can be challenging but what's the alternative? That's right, more of the same. So again, it's your choice.

And then there are those of us who don't have family. If that's you, then friendships are critical to your health and well-being as well as your happiness.

If you're starting from scratch – and very few of us do – I suggest you look at your current friendships and see which ones you can take a little further. True friendships take time to develop because it takes trust to take any relationship to the next level.

The principles described apply not only to your life partner but to all relationships and, especially, to your relationship with yourself.

If your health doesn't allow you to go out and about, how about the internet? Friendships can be made online. Your physical friends can be kept in touch using Skype if they're too far away for a casual visit or, for those who live fairly close, they can come and visit.

It is true that, in life, it sometimes doesn't just rain, it pours. Here's where your mindset becomes vital:

Life's challenges offer a treasure trove of opportunities to develop your resourcefulness, your resilience and your creativity to deal with those setbacks and disappointments.

There's no doubt that some of them are harder than others so, I invite you to look back over your life. If you're 'mature' then you will have had your fair share of failures, setbacks and disappointments.

How did you handle them? How did you survive them? What did you do to overcome them? And, more importantly, what have you learned from the experience?

The best example I can think of, where failure led to huge success, was my own 37-year marriage.

When I finally left, aged 60, I still believed my husband Jim was to blame for my unhappiness. It wasn't until years later that I finally saw the many ways I contributed to my own unhappiness – and his, though he never said. He just withdrew and stopped communicating.

But those insights, painful though they were, paved the way for understanding exactly what does not work in a relationship; they paved the way for this book and, best of all, they actually laid the foundation for the most wonderful relationship I could have imagined with a man who is my friend, my lover, my soulmate.

I was able to look at my failed marriage, learn from my mistakes, rebuild my life and find happiness.

What is the secret to feeling good about yourself?

You feel good about yourself when you truly know yourself. You'd be surprised if you knew how few people do.

You feel good about yourself when you like and trust yourself, and your own judgement.

When you do so, your self-confidence, your self-esteem and your sense of self-worth grow. That means that you know you can handle life's challenges and be creative in the way you approach them. You know you're capable, resilient and resourceful.

From this place of self-knowledge and self-confidence, you know you don't have to remain in pain, you know you can actually take steps to transform your life and your relationships.

You may not believe this so let me be blunt.

You're worthy of being loved, cherished, heard and understood.

This is what I had forgotten all those years ago when I went on that fateful programme, 'Spiritual Renewal' where Miranda Holden took us on that journey towards self-forgiveness, specifically, in my case, to forgive myself for believing I wasn't worthy of being loved.

That's when everything changed for me.

There have been many milestones along the way and I continue to learn and to grow, using everything I learned along the way, and my life keeps getting better and better.

This is what I want for you.

I will take you on a journey, YOUR journey. This is a journey that will enable you to create the life and relationships you want and deserve.

Chapter 4 – How my system was born

"If I create from the heart, nearly everything works; if from the head, almost nothing."
Marc Chagal, French painter, printmaker and designer

As a result of my own experiences, I developed a system I call 'The Ultimate Conscious Loving Formula'.

As you can see, this system has 4 modules.

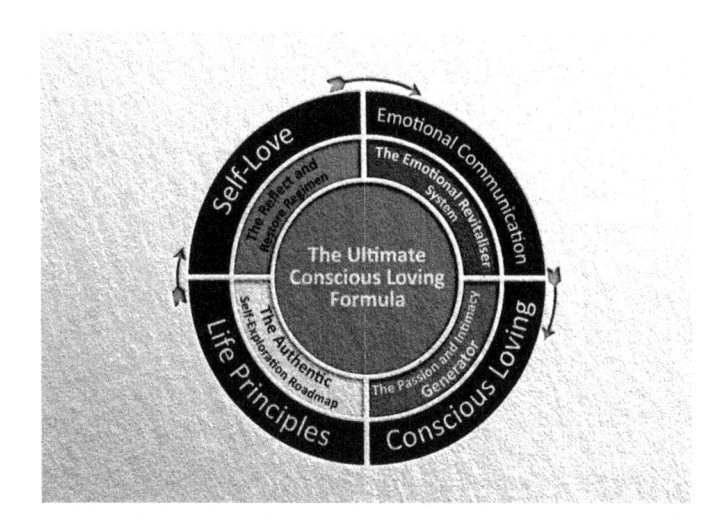

Open Your Heart

The first module looks at **Life Principles** – In this module we identify your mindset, your Gremlin or negative inner critic. We explore your attitudes, values and beliefs that hold you back, that keep you insecure and riddled with self-doubt. And we also explore the many ways you stop yourself from reaching out for what you want the most, and how to change your mindset.

The second module, **Self-Love** – looks at how you allow other people to take you for granted, treat you unkindly and thoughtlessly without you putting a stop to it. In this module, you identify your needs and wants, and learn to have them met. Here you discover how to communicate with another person to enable them to hear you without becoming defensive, and engage with them in a different way, making them change the way they treat you.

The third module is **Emotional Communication** where we explore what makes friendship the foundation of a relationship that is solid and long lasting. This is where you discover attitudes and behaviours you need for building the kind of friendship that will support your relationship well into your old age. Jointly you are then enabled to face the challenges that life sends you.

Finally, the fourth module is **Conscious Loving**. Here you discover what it takes to generate closeness, emotional intimacy and passion which is built on both you and your partner feeling emotionally safe with each other.

'The Ultimate Conscious Loving Formula' was born from the ashes of my pain, anger and disappointment, and gave them meaning.

Working through these four modules is a process that gives you the life tools to build successful relationships where you feel loved, cherished and appreciated.

Love is synonymous with happiness.

Love is synonymous with health and wellbeing.

Love is synonymous with a long life.

Can people make us happy?

As a society, we have been brought up to believe that it is our job to make other people happy and that it is their job to make us happy.

Why is it a problem?

It is a problem because nobody can make us happy nor can we make other people happy. You will often hear people say, "You have to take responsibility for your own feelings. You have to own them."

What does it mean to own your feelings?

It simply means that whether something somebody does makes you feel happy or unhappy depends on how you interpret that particular gesture.

That person may have intended their gesture to make you happy but you may have interpreted it differently.

As for us, we like doing things to make the people we love happy but that can backfire if they don't want or value that gesture. Then we feel rejected, unappreciated and taken for granted. I know I did.

Does that mean we shouldn't do nice things for other people?

Not at all! All it means is that whatever we do for them is because we love them, not because we want them to react in a particular way. That can only lead to disappointment.

The good news is that you're in control of your thoughts which means you can change them – with practice, of course – and when you do, your life and relationships will be transformed.

Only you can decide what to think and how to interpret what happens to you in your life that makes you feel sad or happy.

And here's more good news:

By choosing thoughts and ways to interpret events that make you feel good about yourself you are, at the same time, creating an environment that not only fosters happiness in others but also attracts happy people to you.

How to be happy

To be happy, we first need to have a fulfilling life which includes outside interests such as painting, pottery, joining a book club, learning a language or anything that you may find challenging and satisfying in different ways, close friendships and people you can turn to in times of trouble.

Paul shared with me the extent to which his friends came to his aid when his marriage fell apart. And I, too, had friends to turn to when I was diagnosed with breast cancer.

You don't have to wait for a crisis to strike before turning to a friend, but the friendship, including trust, needs to already exist if and when the crisis strikes.

We also need to have a purpose in our daily life, whatever that might be for you. In other words, something that makes it worthwhile to get out of bed in the morning.

This is more than having something to do – paid or unpaid. It is a feeling that you make a difference. Mine is my work, which is both my passion and my mission. In Paul's case, it is his voluntary work and his gift to make things, including jewellery which gives him huge satisfaction.

For you that might be babysitting your grandchildren to give your daughter a break – or you might even do it for neighbours and friends as well!

The one thing we do NOT need is to depend on somebody else for our happiness. If, for one reason or another, they should no longer be in our life we would have nothing left.

All we can do for each other is enrich each other's lives – without demands, neediness or expectations because, when the expectations we place, especially on our partner, are frustrated, we usually resort to our fall-back behaviours -

blaming, criticising, judging, nagging, manipulating and trying to change them.

This is not just theory. To my shame, this is how I behaved towards Jim, my husband of 37 years. Predictably, it does NOT work. And I'm not alone. My clients too behave in the same way because neither they, nor I, knew what else to do to have our needs met.

We're by no means unique. Such romantic behaviours are widespread – probably because that's how behaviours are portrayed in films and novels, in the media and society in general – plus we see it acted out every day with our parents, families and friends.

So, just because this approach is widespread doesn't mean

(a) that it works or

(b) that you have to follow the herd.

The evidence of this failure is all around you - unhappy couples who stay together for a variety of reasons as well as all the couples who separate or divorce. The number of broken homes and families are a sad testimony to the folly of continuing to engage with your partner as you've always done.

This insight has made a huge difference to my relationship with Paul because I finally understood that behaving as I did in my marriage never got me what I so yearned for – to love and be loved wholeheartedly.

What I came to see is that it's only in our relationship with our partner, our children and our parents that we try to control them through demands, neediness, guilt trips and expectations.

If you stop and consider this you will realise that we don't do this with our friends. We wouldn't dream of laying guilt on them, having expectations, nagging them or trying to change or control them – so why do we do it with our primary relationships?

I think the answer is because we have a lot more invested in them.

The point of my system, 'The Ultimate Conscious Loving Formula', is that it shows you how to build the relationship you long for.

When you look at your life and your relationship, do you catch yourself thinking any of these thoughts?

"This is how it is and there's nothing I can do about it."

"Is this all there is?"

"Am I being ungrateful for wanting more?"

"There HAS to be another way – I just wish I knew what that way was!"

The good news is that you have within you all the resources you need with which to build the life and relationships you really want.

The bad news is that those resources are buried under heaps and heaps of limiting beliefs, self-criticism, low self-confidence, poor self-esteem and a very poor sense of self-worth.

Without realising you were doing it *you* have been creating the life and relationships you currently have with both the parts of your life you like and the parts of your life you don't like.

There is no random, cruel force out there or people who deliberately conspire to make you feel unhappy or frustrated.

The sheer inconsistency of your decision-making means that the results have tended to be unpredictable, sometimes unexpected and often unwelcome.

Like many other people, you have lived on automatic pilot, doing what you always did, reacting in the same way, even in new situations – without wondering or questioning – living from a place of habit and responding to situations with the same knee-jerk reactions.

It's not really surprising that you have done so. Evolutionary psychologists have found that we're programmed to repeatedly think, feel, say and do the many of the same things, over and over again even when they don't benefit us.

I'm no exception, or I wasn't until I embarked on the journey which brought me here today, able to share with you how I got here.

When I chose the title of my book - 'Open Your Heart' - I thought of it in terms of not only opening your heart to your partner, your family, your friends, your community even, but also opening your heart to yourself.

The purpose of this book is to show you how to become more self-aware so you can create – *consciously and deliberately* – the life and relationship you always wanted.

I'm often asked, "Transforming a relationship is a huge challenge, so how can you guarantee success?"

This is a valid question and I'm afraid I have to tell you that there are no guarantees.

What I *can* tell you is that your relationship will change when you decide that relationships are reciprocal, that is to say, give and take, and not just giving and giving and giving, something far too many women are brought up to do – myself included, and often men as well even though no-one asked me to do so or, worse still, even though they didn't even want it in the first place!

Your relationships will change when you decide to take control of your own choices. And you will begin to make choices that really work for you when you have reached a place where you really know yourself, when you really know what you need and want, what's really true for you and what really matters to you. And, most importantly of all, you will make choices that really work for you when you like, trust and respect yourself.

Your relationships will change when you decide to expect to be treated with consideration and kindness, and when you learn how to make that happen.

And finally, your relationships will change when you begin to take the smallest step that will bring you the greatest results. In other words, you will succeed in changing your life and your relationships when you begin to take consistent baby steps.

Here I will show you what those baby steps are and how to put them into practice.

These are the barriers my clients have often placed in their own way until they decided it's time to seek help. Is this you?

They're afraid to make themselves emotionally vulnerable

Top of the list of desires my clients bring to me is to have an intimate relationship. What stops them from having what they want is that intimacy requires us to make ourselves emotionally vulnerable. Protecting ourselves from possibly being hurt or rejected only keeps love at arm's length. But making ourselves emotionally vulnerable takes courage because it feels risky and scary. That's why it's so important to like and respect yourself.

They're afraid to admit being wrong

For most of my adult life I needed to be right – at whatever the cost. I chose being right over being happy. To do otherwise felt like admitting I got it wrong most of my adult life. It was one of the nails in the coffin of my marriage.

They have fallen into the habit of focusing on the things that irritate and frustrate them about their partner

Part of my need to be right was the habit of focusing on the things that irritated me about Jim. It was a habit that made me lose sight of the things I loved and appreciated about him when we first got together.

They're afraid to express their feelings, especially when they're hurt or upset

I used to believe that being truthful about what I really felt would rock the boat and bring into the open things that made me feel resentful or hurt. I was convinced that it would only make things worse.

In reality, the opposite was true. Keeping my resentments and hurts to myself made things worse because, by remaining unexpressed, they ended up turning into anger.

That was something I tried to hide, even from myself. It was a high price to pay for such a distorted belief.

They believe it's selfish to want more

This was one of my main limiting beliefs, that doing enjoyable things for myself or asking for what I wanted was selfish.

This was a belief that was drummed into me by my parents, my mum in particular.

Both of them were convinced that it was essential for me to do whatever it took to be liked because, they believed, my survival depended on it – and asking for what you wanted flew in the face of this conviction.

These are all fears based on the belief that you're unworthy of love and happiness – a belief people are usually totally unaware of – as was I.

Chapter 5 – Getting started: keep a journal

> *"A personal journal is an ideal environment in which to 'become'. It is a perfect place for you to think, feel, discover, expand, remember, and dream."*
> Brad Wilcox, educationalist and academic

Keeping a journal allows you to clarify your thoughts and feelings enabling you to get to know yourself.

It helps you pour your experiences from inside your head on to paper. You begin to see things more clearly. In turn, this will help reduce your levels of stress, confusion and anxiety.

After keeping a journal for some time you will start recognising habits and patterns which negatively affect the quality of your life and relationships.

Step 1

Buy a notebook that is as attractive as possible to reflect the importance of your journey. If you live in the UK, you might like to check out Paperchase or Muji.

Step 2

Write down everything you notice – your thoughts, your feelings, what you say and do, and how it works out for you.

For example, when something happens that makes you feel hurt, angry or upset, what do you tell yourself? That the other person is to blame, that everything is so unfair or that it's not your fault?

When you know what you need to do to make positive changes and tell yourself "I can't do that!", write that down. That's a limiting belief. The truth is, you don't *want* to do that. It's a choice. And you can always change your mind about the choices you make.

Step 3

Write down your thoughts, your feelings, your ideas, insights, memories, values and beliefs, and everything you feel you want to record and remember.

Step 4

Focus on the physical sensations in your body, which is where your feelings are located.

For example, if you feel slightly nauseous, perhaps you're feeling anxious; if your jaw is tight or your fists are clenched, perhaps you're feeling angry and trying not to show it. If you're sitting slumped, perhaps you're feeling discouraged. Alternatively, if you're sitting upright with your head held high, you might be feeling really good or, if you feel a light fluttering sensation in your tummy, you might be feeling really happy.

Get to know the sensations in your body.

Step 5

Notice and record when you're struggling, resisting, blaming or feeling reluctant or defensive.

Notice your excuses and justifications, for example, "I'm too busy to do these exercises." Or "This is stupid. It's all nonsense anyway." Or "It'll never work. My habits are far too entrenched."

Also, whenever you try something new, record how it went.

Chapter 6 – Begin your journey

"I've done stupid things and made poor choices but that's all been part of my journey, and I have learned from my mistakes."
Sue Plumtree

Before you can transform your relationship or any other area in your life, you need to know what you actually want. Think of this as planning a holiday.

Knowing what you want or where you want to be gives you a sense of direction.

To support you in this, I have listed below a series of questions that will enable you to start the transformation process. Write the answers down in your journal.

These questions are courtesy of the book 'The Seven Levels Of Intimacy: The Art of Loving and the Joy of Being Loved', by Matthew Kelly.

These questions are useful whether you're single or in a relationship.

Exercise

Make a list of your needs and wants. Be as specific as possible. If, for example, you write down, "I need to be supported" add what exactly would make you feel supported.

Now ask yourself: "Which of my needs and wants can I meet myself?"

For example, if you have a need to feel better about yourself, start by treating yourself better – a walk in the park, a break in your routine (even 5 minutes fresh air will help), a bubble bath, time out to read a favourite book or just listen to music without doing anything else.

"Which ones can I reasonably expect my partner (or somebody else) to meet?"

For example, if you both work full time, it is reasonable to expect that you share the household chores.

"Which need(s) is/are non-negotiable, the deal-breakers? Which ones will I not compromise on?"

To identify this one, ask yourself, "When I suffer most, which need is not being met?"

And resolve to never be in this position again whether in your current relationship or in a new one, if you're currently unattached.

Don't worry if the answers don't come to you all at once. Keep thinking about them as you go about your daily life. The answers *will* emerge, so I suggest you keep a little notebook with you at all times, just in case.

Chapter 7 – Life Principles – The Authentic Self-Exploration Roadmap

Secret No. 1: To change your life you need to become self-aware

> *"Watch your thoughts; they become words.*
> *Watch your words; they become actions.*
> *Watch your actions; they become habits.*
> *Watch your habits; they become character.*
> *Watch your character; it becomes your destiny."*
> Lao Tzu, ancient Chinese philosopher and writer

Becoming self-aware is essential if you want to make changes in your life and your relationships. If you don't know what you're doing that either works or does not work for you, how can you change things?

Self-awareness gives you a simple choice:

To carry on as you are or create something new based on your true needs and wants.

Here's the thing:

Until you become more self-aware, you will continue to create a life that is more disappointing than fulfilling. That's why continuing to live on automatic pilot, from a place of habit, will seriously harm your chances of being happy.

Living on automatic pilot

As I said in Truth No. 1 in the Introduction, you have jointly created your relationships, even the circumstances of your life. The problem is that you have done so from a place of habit which means that you didn't realise you were doing it.

If this is you, you may find this a hard truth to face. However, when you stop resisting, defending and blaming, you will realise just how liberating this insight is.

Up until now, you've been living your life from a place of habit without ever wondering or questioning any of it.

Here are some of the habits I used to have. They fell into two categories:

- habits in my relationship with others, in particular with Jim
- habits in my relationship with myself.

Habits in my relationship with Jim

I was determined to be right at all costs, even at the cost of my own happiness.

I blamed him for my unhappiness and everything that was wrong in our marriage.

I was 'a fixer and a rescuer', doing things for him that he should have been doing himself.

My worst excess was during a period when he'd been made redundant. I used to go to the library to find job adverts that I regarded as suitable, then I would write the CV and the covering letter. All he had to do was sign it. If I could have gone to the job interview in his place, I would even have done that.

Obviously, that's control-freakery at its most extreme. Sadly, I never saw it at the time. That's how, over time, I came to disempower him.

But I wasn't the only one to blame for this. Jim allowed me to do this and never stood up to say "Wait a minute!" Instead he became passive-aggressive, the only way he knew how to protect himself.

I used to expect him to know what I wanted without me having to tell him. When I didn't get what I wanted, I'd feel angry and resentful and accuse him of not loving me.

Habits in my relationship with myself

I deceived myself about all sorts of things.

- What I really felt – because I thought it would put people off. That's why I presented a perpetually cheerful mask.

- What I really needed and wanted – because I didn't believe I deserved it.

- What was really true for me. For example, I pretended to be happy – because I couldn't face the depth of my unhappiness.

And all the time I wondered why I felt unloved – as if I'd had nothing to do with it.

Until I became more self-aware, I hadn't realised that it was the quality of my thoughts and beliefs that affected my relationship with myself and others.

The blame game

One of my habits which, as I discovered later, is actually fairly common, was blaming other people for whatever made me feel unhappy and resentful.

If this is you, then it's really important that you make it a top priority to let go of the 'blame game'.

What does 'letting go of the blame game' look like in practice?

Here's an example.

While I was still married to Jim, I blamed him for purposely behaving the way he did to make me unhappy. I also told myself that he did everything he said or did not say, and everything he did or did not do intentionally, just to wind me up.

Don't get me wrong. I wasn't entirely mistaken but the point is this:

Without realising it, I made myself out to be 'the innocent bystander'.

I told myself he was thoughtless, unkind, unreliable and totally unable or unwilling to engage with me in the way I needed him to. I also told myself that, in contrast to him, I was always kind, loving, supportive and thoughtful.

This next point is so important that you need to record it in your journal.

All relationships are created jointly.

This means, to use a colloquialism, that it 'takes two to tango'.

Once you let go of the 'blame game', you will realise that this is where your power lies, by taking responsibility for your own happiness and for your part in the equation.

That's because, if you want to change or revitalise your relationship, you can only change yourself, specifically your thoughts and your behaviours. This is where your true power lies.

There are two ways you can get another person to change:

- If they're willing and able to do so, and all you have to do is ask.
- When you change the way you engage with them.

How to do the second way is the subject of a later chapter but, right now, you need to accept that, unless you change the way you communicate, nothing will work, no matter how hard you try. And you will feel as if you were hitting your head against a brick wall.

Believe me. I know. I tried it for 37 years.

How life works

The remainder of this chapter and the next one shows you how to start the process of changing your relationship with yourself.

Let's begin with a very simplistic description of how life in general and relationships in particular actually work:

Your thoughts affect your feelings and your feelings affect everything you say and do.

You might ask: "Is this it?"

Well, yes and no. As you'd expect, it's more complicated than that.

First, you need to understand three things.

Before you can make any changes you need to, as I mentioned earlier, get to know yourself.

To know yourself, you need to get to understand your mindset and the story you tell yourself about yourself, about other people and about life in general.

To discover your mindset and the story you tell yourself, you need to start noticing your thoughts – which is where the cycle begins.

How to get to know yourself

Your journal is an important resource to help you with this. (See Chapter 5 – 'Getting Started: Keep A Journal')

Do regular reality checks. Check if your current beliefs are still valid. Is this belief opinion or fact? What is the evidence? What does your heart call you to do? Do your experiences with people match or differ from your beliefs about how they should be? Do you tend to enjoy their company or are you usually frustrated when you're with them?

Continuing on your journey to get to know yourself, you need to become aware of what your needs and wants really are, even though your Gremlin or, in other words, your negative inner critic, will try to make you feel selfish for wanting something for yourself.

People differ in the way they experience love which means that we or our partner may or may not recognise a particular gesture as loving.

That's because everybody has a different way of expressing or experiencing love.

I learned how to express love by looking at what my parents did that worked so well for them.

I assumed it would work equally well with Jim but I couldn't have been more wrong. And he certainly didn't respond in the way I hoped.

As for his way of expressing love, sadly, I didn't experience it as love so I felt unloved.

It is really important you know what makes you feel loved. Which of these behaviours make you feel most loved?

He often tells you how much he loves you.

When you're together, your partner is really with you, not on their device checking messages.

They really listen to you and remember what you said.

They make you a priority in their life or, at least, equally important to their other priorities, including work.

They may, occasionally, bring you a gift. What kind of gift is less important other than it should be something they know you will like. For you, gifts are evidence that they were thinking of you.

They treat you with tenderness, give you a hug, a gentle caress or a kiss – all signs of affection.

They do things for you to ease the burden, lending a hand or helping out. This is where the saying comes in, "actions speak louder than words."

I suggest you make a list of what makes you feel loved and put it in order of importance to you.

Being clear what makes you feel loved is absolutely critical because it will enable you to ask for what you really need and want.

Don't for one minute believe that, if they really love you, they'd know. Many people, usually women, believe that if you have to ask it doesn't count.

This is absolute nonsense. It's when you ask repeatedly and they don't take it on board that alarm bells should be ringing.

Getting to know yourself is the foundation that will enable you to create a new life experience because, until that point, your choices and decisions will continue to be more like knee-jerk reactions and therefore, not always right for you.

Once you get to know yourself you will begin to trust yourself to make choices that work for you a whole lot better.

As the process continues and you get to know yourself more and more you will learn to like yourself and then trust yourself to make changes that work for you.

This alone will enable you to move from a place where perhaps you feel helpless, hopeless, resigned, anxious and negative to one where you feel more confident, positive and resilient. That's because you will discover that you're more capable and resourceful than you ever believed you were.

How do you get to like yourself?

You might wonder how you get from knowing yourself to liking yourself when you didn't before.

The truth is it takes time.

In my own case, the process started with the realisation that I deserved to be happy. That was the moment when everything changed. As I set off on my journey, it soon became clear that it wasn't going to be easy – and yet I stayed with it.

When I looked at myself after a few months having kept records of my progress in my journal, I saw a woman who'd had the courage to face difficult realities, especially about herself, and do something about them.

She forgave herself when she fell back, she saw how she picked herself up and carried on despite the setbacks. And she liked what she saw. That woman was me and that's how I began to get to like myself.

You might say it was and is, a mixture of courage, determination, self-forgiveness, self-respect and self-compassion.

A good starting point for making changes is to examine your mindset.

What is a mindset?

Your mindset is composed of your thoughts, attitudes, values and beliefs which help shape the story you tell yourself about yourself – about who you are. They also shape the story you tell yourself about how other people are. They even shape the story you tell yourself about how life works.

For example, you might tell yourself that you're not good at something, that you're too old (or too young, or too fat or too thin or too short or too tall – whatever).

You might tell yourself you're too tired to do something you know you need to do and that watching the telly would make you feel better or more relaxed.

You might tell yourself that people are selfish – or loving and generous. You might tell yourself, life is what you make it or you might tell yourself there's no point trying because nothing works anyway.

The beliefs you hold about yourself includes what you can and cannot do, what is and is not possible or how you believe people will respond. In other words, your mindset pre-determines your reactions, responses and how you interpret everything that happens to you.

Those beliefs make you behave in a way that creates your experience.

There are, in fact, two different mindsets.

Fixed Mindset. People with a fixed mindset believe that their qualities are set in stone. Things are the way they are and there's nothing they can do about it. Things just happen to them. Their talents and gifts are whatever they're born with and that's it. They tend to worry about whether they're good enough. They tend to have something to prove to themselves and others. They tend to be perfectionists. Of course, this is a never-ending struggle.

Flexible Mindset. People with a flexible mindset tend to regard their qualities as things that can be developed and expanded if they put their mind to it, for example, by going on courses, travelling, experimenting, reading and learning new things. In short, they're willing to push beyond their comfort zone. They believe in 'feeling the fear and doing it anyway.'

Our mindsets are expressed through our thoughts and, as mentioned above, our thoughts affect our feelings, and our feelings affect everything we say and do, including our choices and decisions. For example, when it comes to the story we tell ourselves about ourselves, are we the victim or are we the hero of our story?

Most of us are quite unaware that our thoughts are the expression of our values and beliefs. So, ideally, if we want to become more self-aware, we need to start by noticing which thought brought up a particular feeling.

However, this isn't as easy as it sounds because, according to the Laboratory of Neuro Imaging, we think about 70,000 thoughts per day which means they usually flit through our mind too fast to grab hold of.

A better way is to focus on the physical sensations in our body because that's where our feelings live. That makes them easier to recognise.

Here are some examples.

A faint nauseous sensation around your tummy might mean you're feeling anxious.

Gritted teeth or clenched fists might mean you're feeling angry.

A headache might mean you're feeling stressed.

How I changed my mindset

I spent most of my adult life trapped in a fixed mindset.

I just 'knew' that my life would always be as it was and that there was nothing I could do to change it.

I felt hopeless and impotent.

The change from fixed to flexible mindset was gradual.

Over time I became more self-aware so, little by little, I started noticing my habits and patterns.

I also started trying out new things, to experiment, to see what I liked and what I didn't like, to see what worked for me and what didn't.

Over time I started noticing that most choices were not cast in stone and that it wouldn't be the end of the world if whatever I tried didn't work out. I could always change my mind and try something else. How liberating is that!

This is something you can try for yourself. Trying out new things may feel risky, but making any sort of change requires you to push beyond your comfort zone, if you want something better for yourself.

The idea is to dip your toe into the water, not to jump right in.

Secret No. 2 – The Gremlin is at the root of your unhappiness

> *"Your primary cause of unhappiness is never the situation but your thoughts about it."*
> *Eckhart Tolle*

The first time I discovered I had something that coaches call a Gremlin or negative inner critic, was when I started my coaching training.

I also discovered that this inner dialogue starts from the moment we wake up until the moment we fall asleep.

The problem is, most people don't realise this is going on, a kind of running commentary that runs through our mind 24/7 about everything that's happening, both within and outside of ourselves.

The Gremlin's intention is to make us feel bad or insecure about ourselves.

When the subject of the Gremlin came up on my course, I began to notice how, to use a colloquialism, I'd beat myself up, compare myself with other people – always the ones I regarded as more talented, more successful, more popular, more beautiful, slimmer and/or luckier.

Believing I wasn't good enough spilled over into other areas of my life.

Until that fateful moment when I decided I deserved to be happy, every time I wanted to take a risk that might lead to greater happiness and fulfilment, the Gremlin would flood me with fear and self-doubt.

The fact that I became a chameleon, a people-pleaser, was a direct result of not just listening to the damning whispers of my Gremlin but, worse, believing everything it said.

It was my negative inner dialogue that caused me to tolerate unacceptable and unkind behaviours, and make choices that cost me my happiness, my health and my wellbeing.

Over the years, I became depressed and overweight. I then developed bulimia, a severe eating disorder that could have proven fatal if I hadn't known somewhere deep inside of me I didn't want to die.

The science behind the Gremlin

The concept of the 'critical inner dialogue' is based on scientific research, which has established that this is not a personal but a universal condition, one that scientists call 'inner speech'.

Originally, its purpose was to quickly detect threats in the environment so you could decide whether to fight or flee.

As long as the threat is physical, that's a valid response but, when the threat is of an emotional nature, your body heats up and this increased energy has nowhere to go.

This causes the body to release adrenalin and the hormone cortisol which increases stress levels and mobilises the strength needed to confront the threat. However, if the threat is non-existent, it will have no way of releasing these chemicals naturally through the body and, instead, they build up and affect you physically and emotionally.

Nowadays, such threats are not always real; sometimes it's the Gremlin that makes them appear real, for example, emotional attacks, either from ourselves (as when we 'beat ourselves up') or from others, for example, when we allow someone to cross the line by acting thoughtlessly, rudely, unkindly, carelessly or generally unacceptably – and let them get away with it.

Our Gremlin floods us with negative messages – not only continually reminding us that we're not good enough, but also pointing out all the things that can go wrong if we want to try something new or making us feel selfish for wanting something for ourselves.

Here are two important facts you need to know about the Gremlin.

You will never be able to eliminate it because it is hard-wired into the oldest part of our brain called the reptilian brain.

You can learn to manage it. Here's an analogy: imagine a beautiful garden. To keep it looking lovely you need to remove the weeds – not once and for all, but regularly. It's the same with the negative thoughts the Gremlin tries to bombard you with.

Open Your Heart

How to manage your Gremlin

Exercise 1

Buy two little figures – one, a horrible monster and the other, a harmless-looking figure and put them where you can see them. You can buy them in toy shops.

Transfer your negative and critical thoughts from inside your head to the horrible monster.

This monster will be rough on you but now, instead of you thinking "*Who do I think I am, wanting (whatever)!*" – you will hear your Gremlin telling you "*Who do YOU think you are to want (whatever)!*" or instead of thinking *"I'm stupid!"* you will hear your Gremlin telling you, *"YOU are stupid!"* which is easier to notice and challenge.

Having said that, it may take time because, in the beginning, you may continue to believe these messages; after all, you've believed them all your life. Even if you do, there will come a point when you will notice and challenge them.

"Wait a minute!", you might say to yourself, "This is rubbish! I want this and I *can* do this! I may have to learn how but that's not a problem!"

The second Gremlin, the harmless-looking one, is actually far more dangerous than the ugly monster because the messages sound so reasonable.

For example, imagine you want to lose weight and you're actually making good progress.

But then you go to meet a friend and she urges you to have a slice of chocolate cake. You first try telling her you shouldn't because you're on a diet but she persists until you give in. Afterwards you feel really bad about yourself and start beating yourself up for having been so weak.

That's the work of the Gremlin.

Benefits of transferring your negative inner dialogue on to the little figures

There are two huge advantages of using the little figurines.

Externalising your Gremlin allows you to recognise it more easily and, from there, to challenge it.

Because, as you will see below, your negative and critical thoughts are one of five types of thoughts, what you're doing is taking only your negative and critical thoughts out of the mix. All your other thoughts will continue to enable you to function normally, for example planning, analysing, remembering, enjoying, creating, and so on.

Clients often ask me, "How do I know which thoughts are mine and which belong to my Gremlin?"

I tell them, "Thoughts that make you feel good about yourself are yours. Thoughts that make you feel not good about yourself are the Gremlin's."

Exercise 2

When your Gremlin is being particularly rough or devious, try this.

Imagine a young child, say six or seven years old. It's upset, crying and giving itself a really hard time.

What would you say to that child? Would you shake them and shout at them or would you comfort and reassure?

Write down your observations and your insights in your journal.

Limiting beliefs

I lived a large part of my adult life treating myself critically, hurtfully. I 'knew' I wasn't good enough and that I needed to be whatever I believed other people wanted me to be so they would like me, accept me and be acceptable.

Those are the beliefs of a committed 'people-pleaser', as I used to be.

Depending on whether your beliefs are similar or different from mine, then so will be your behaviours.

After you've been paying attention for a while and have started noticing them, I suggest you write them down in your journal.

Over time you will begin to recognise your habits and patterns, something you can't see when you move unconsciously from moment to moment.

Here are some examples of behaviours that were driven by my thoughts. These thoughts were determined by my beliefs about myself and they damaged me so deeply that I ended up not knowing who I really was:

I'd blame myself and 'beat myself up' for just about everything.

I'd put everybody else's needs ahead of mine, telling myself that doing otherwise would be selfish – that was my Mum's voice whispering to me.

I was reluctant to ask for what I needed and wanted, believing I didn't deserve it.

I found it really hard to accept compliments.

I never spoke out when somebody said something that upset me because I was afraid of rocking the boat.

I believed I wasn't good enough.

I ignored my sensible inner voice or inner wisdom.

I didn't believe I was lovable.

I didn't trust my own judgement usually believing that other people knew better.

I compared myself negatively with others.

Do any of these chime with you?

Types of thoughts

I normally encourage my clients to try and grab hold of the thought that triggers a particular feeling because our behaviours are triggered by our feelings – and those behaviours cause people to react and respond in a particular way.

If those thoughts, feelings and behaviours are consistent they will shape the tone of all our relationships – both the one with ourselves and the one with others.

And we not only shape our relationships, we also shape our present and our future through the choices we make now.

But, grabbing hold of any one particular thought, negative or otherwise, is difficult because there are so many different types all mixed up together in our head.

Some wise person has taken the trouble to classify our thoughts and put them into four distinct categories:

Positive thoughts, for example, "I love walking in the park!", "Jane is coming over; we have a lot of catching up to do!", and so on.

Neutral thoughts, for example, "I need to get to the supermarket!", "I need to check the time of my appointment" and so on.

Wasteful thoughts. There are two types of wasteful thoughts: worry and guilt.

Worry: "Oh dear, Fred is 10 minutes late! There must have been an accident!" or "I keep forgetting things! I'm sure this must be the onset of Alzheimers!"

Guilt: "I shouldn't have had that bar of chocolate!" "I really shouldn't feel happy when John is miserable!"

Negative thoughts – that's your Gremlin that you've now transferred on to the little figurines.

And here's the thing:

Because, as I explained before, we live our life out of habit we're not aware of our thoughts nor are we aware that this is how we create our life experience.

One of the things about negative thoughts is that we tend to put an interpretation on events. Nothing that happens to you, including what people say and do has any meaning …

… except for the meaning you decide it has.

Here are some examples of common thoughts that could have a variety of interpretations although we, typically, tend to choose the negative one:

- "Jack said that to upset me."

- "Jenny walked right past me because she's a snotty bitch."

- "My manager just gave me a negative appraisal. It's obvious she has it in for me."

Open Your Heart

These are the type of thoughts that make you feel insecure, angry, upset or resentful and, when you are in that space, your choices and your actions will reflect those feelings. Furthermore, your focus narrows to the point where your options become so constricted that you can't see the other possibilities available to you.

How we create our life in general and our relationships in particular

Outdated beliefs expressed through negative thoughts are a great example of how they continue to make us create the life and relationships we insist we do not want. And we rarely, if ever, question how we're doing this.

But negative thoughts are not the only way we create our life. After all, challenges, disappointments, setbacks and failures are all part of our everyday life experience.

While this is a human response, far too many people stay in that negative space and tell themselves the story that there's obviously no point in carrying on or trying again.

Other people, on the other hand, will have learnt from past unhappy experiences and are willing to try again. They will be the ones who are able to build a new loving and solid relationship.

Perceptions and interpretations

When you start paying more attention to your feelings, you will notice how quickly they go up and down, as your day progresses.

You will experience a series of events which will affect your mood more than you realise – every person you encounter, every small happening as the day unfolds will have an impact on your mood.

Instead of letting yourself be swept up and down by random emotions, start paying attention and record not only what is happening but also how those events make you feel and how you respond.

Try to see if you can pinpoint the particular thought which started that rollercoaster of emotions. This is important because – and it bears repeating:

It doesn't matter what happens to you; what matters is how you REACT AND RESPOND to what happens to you.

You can trigger any emotion with just a thought. It could be something as subtle as, "Shit!" or "Cool!"

That's where perceptions and interpretations come in.

Here's a personal example.

I was married 37 years. Many of those years I felt unhappy, unseen, unimportant and unloved. Not exactly a barrel of laughs! I didn't leave until I was 60.

I'm often asked why I waited so long to leave my marriage. This is a valid question.

I have no simple answer. Looking back, it was a combination of being in denial, of playing down my unhappiness, of being unable to imagine myself living on my own, of believing myself incapable of handling the stuff Jim did and a lot of fear of the unknown all mixed in.

I left when I finally decided I deserved better, that I deserved to be happy, that I deserved to be loved – plus the fact that the pain of staying was worse than the fear of the unknown.

At that point I felt ready to take this life-changing step.

I'm keen to make this clear because there are far too many people who are unhappy in their relationship yet feel unable to leave, blaming themselves for their lack of courage.

Yet, I don't regret having waited as long as I did. Why?

One reason is timing. When you're ready, you're ready.

The other reason is the fact that it took that long for me to become the woman who would feel confident enough to leave her marriage of 37 years and build a new life for herself, a life that included writing her autobiography, establish a successful life coaching practice, attracting open-hearted and loving friendships, and discovering new talents and gifts along the way.

In the 12 years that followed I learned what mistakes I made in my marriage that contributed to it breaking up. This was a truly liberating insight because it enabled me to take responsibility for my part in it. Up until that point, I continued to blame Jim for everything that went wrong and that made me into a victim.

Recognising the role I played meant I could change myself. Having done that I am now able to use everything I learned for the benefit of my relationship with the man who turned out to be the love of my life.

I learned the hard way what destroys a relationship, exactly what makes it work and how to create the trust and emotional safety that deepens love, passion and intimacy.

Without having experienced the pain in my marriage I would not have learned the things I have that I'm now able to share with you. I wouldn't have become a writer. I wouldn't be doing work I'm passionate about. I wouldn't have the wonderful friendships I have and I wouldn't have developed *The Ultimate Conscious Loving Formula* which empowers and enables thousands of people to build successful relationships where they feel loved, valued and appreciated.

As for you, here are some examples of what your own habits and patterns might bring you.

- You constantly go for the same kind of person, for example one who cheats on you or is cold and distant or is clingy and pretends to be helpless.

- You go for married people because they're 'safe', unlikely to leave their marriage or relationship so you don't have to make a commitment.

- You comfort eat or drink excessively.

- You start fights even when you promised yourself you wouldn't.

- You give, give and give, get very little back, then feel resentful, and so on.

And all the time you wonder why this is always 'happening' to you as if you had nothing to do with it.

In summary

Until you notice your habits and patterns, your thoughts, what you say and do, the choices you make and whether or not they're right for you, you won't be able to make any changes.

As I mentioned under Truth No. 3 in the Introduction, words create reality.

The story you tell yourself – about yourself, about other people and about life in general – is where you focus your energy.

For example, in the context of your relationship, do you tend to focus on the things that irritate you about your partner or do you tend to focus on the things you like and admire about them?

How you stop yourself from moving forwards

Here are some questions you might like to reflect on.

What do you tell yourself ...

- to explain why you're not doing what you know would bring you what you want
- to make it OK to be mercilessly critical of yourself
- to make it OK to allow people to treat you unkindly without putting a stop to it
- to make it OK for you to keep giving without getting much back in return
- to keep saying 'yes' to people's demands when you're already overloaded?

Remember: when you change the story you tell yourself about yourself, about other people and about life in general, you change not only your relationships but also how you experience your own reality.

Chapter 8 – The Reflect and Restore Regimen

Secret No. 3: Self-respect is the magic answer to happy relationships

> *"Respect is as important as love in a relationship."*
> Anon.

How I nearly destroyed any chance of happiness

If you'd been with me on 30 October 1965, you would have found me at the Goethe Institute in London. There's a concert scheduled this evening. The room is small – more like a very large meeting room, and it has no stage. The instruments are all set up – this evening it's going to be a quartet and I'm really looking forward to it.

I arrive early and see that it's completely empty – except for one man sitting in the centre of the room.

I place myself right next to him – a very un-British thing to do but I've only been in England just over 3 months so I have no idea how many social and cultural rules I'm breaking.

I like the look of him, but I judge his hair to be far too long – it reaches all the way to the top of his shirt collar.

The fact that this is the Swinging Sixties has not penetrated my consciousness. I don't even know what it is.

I'm judging his appearance by Argentinian standards, having grown up in Argentina, so I decide that, if I get to know him better, I will persuade him to have his hair cut.

That was the first time I thought there was something about him that I would change and I hadn't even engaged him in conversation yet!

Fast forward one month. It's November now and we've met a couple of times.

I've never been a particularly secure young woman. I'm not sure I'm pretty enough, lovable enough, attractive enough so I decide to see if I can make him fall in love with me.

If I succeed, that will be evidence that I am all those things which I doubt about myself - lovable and attractive.

I've read enough women's magazines to have an idea of how to go about it.

Fast forward to another day. Today is 4 June 2004 and Jim – that's his name – and I are about to part company. We've been married 37 years and, for most of those years I've felt unloved, lonely and unimportant. I've reached the stage where I just can't stand it anymore.

I fleetingly wonder if steamrolling him into a relationship just to prove my attractiveness was too high a price to pay.

How I became the woman who would go to such lengths

As a child, my parents tried hard to bolster my low self-confidence by telling me over and over again how pretty and smart I was.

Unfortunately, I never believed them because, when I was in bed and they thought I was asleep, they would talk about me, worried because they didn't really understand me.

I would lie in bed in the dark, listening to them talk and I knew that, what they really believed was that I wasn't as smart or as pretty, as they said. As a result, I came to believe that I was a disappointment to them.

They also made it clear that it was essential I did whatever it took to get people to like me because, they insisted, my security and wellbeing depended on that. As a result, I turned myself inside out to be whatever I believed people wanted me to be.

In an effort to be appealing, I never did or said anything I thought might put people off. I never stood up for myself. I never put a stop to unacceptable behaviour. And I never said or did anything that might 'rock the boat'.

In short, I twisted myself into a pretzel trying to be all things to all people, a strategy that was doomed to fail.

I also went to great lengths to hide my true feelings and, instead, project a persona that was charming, bubbly and cheerful until I came to believe that the image I projected was who I really was.

Never being sure I was good enough ate away at my self-confidence, my self-esteem and my sense of self-worth. I was continually overwhelmed with self-doubts all of which troubled me for most of my adult life until I turned 56. That was when I started working with Alan, the man who became my life coach.

How I changed my self-perception

This is what I discovered through working with Alan.

Changing my self-perception is an ongoing process, not a destination.

In my case, I changed my self-perception in tiny stages whenever I did something that I'd never done before. Here's a snapshot of my journey.

I try something new and it doesn't work. I torture myself. "I'm slow", "I'm stupid", "I'll never get it", "I'm just not capable or good enough", "Why bother, I'm banging my head against a brick wall", and so on – that's what I told myself. My self-esteem takes a dive.

I try something new and it doesn't work – at least not the first time, or the second or even the third – but I persist and, eventually, I get it! My self-esteem looks up. "This is so unlike me!", I tell myself.

I try something else and it works. "This is so unlike me!", I tell myself again.

I try something new and it works yet again! – My self-esteem and my self-perception take a leap upwards. "I guess this is who I am now", I tell myself.

I decide to lose a couple of pounds to adjust my appearance to my slowly growing self-confidence. I feel great! Friends comment approvingly. I start doing things that I enjoy; small things so as not to upset Jim.

I put on a pound and I beat myself up. I lose it again and I feel incredibly relieved. I vow not to fall off the food wagon again!

There are days when I feel good about myself, although I'm still plagued by other days when I feel as if I've forgotten everything I learned.

Two steps forwards; one step back. The secret is to persist. I persist.

And here's the good news: there comes a point when the momentum of small successes takes over and you just can't give up. Success feeds on success.

This is what I learned:

Self-perception is what you tell yourself about yourself, how you interpret what you said or did. For example, you might re-interpret it from "I'll never get it" to "OK, round one didn't work. What can I do instead?"

And that's a choice. The same principle applies when it comes to choosing the right partner, having made poor choices in the past.

Back to basics – how to recognise the right partner for you

I was talking with a friend the other day. She was telling me about how her daughter's fairly new relationship was going through a rough patch. She didn't think it was going to last.

I suggested that she might choose better next time. My friend replied, "The problem is that you don't know until much later whether you chose well or not."

That got me thinking about whether or not I agreed with her and, on reflection, I didn't.

All I have for evidence is my relationship with Paul, the love of my life.

Could it happen to you too? I think so. I believe my insights could safely be generalised, at least to some extent:

By the time I met Paul, aged 70, I'd come to know myself quite well. Knowing yourself is a pre-condition if you want to recognise the right person for you.

Some of my insights come from my reflections about my long marriage to Jim. After I left, I looked back on our dysfunctional life together because I wanted to understand why I felt so unhappy, what was missing for me and why I felt so unloved.

Over the years my needs and wants had changed. Today I've become more aware of what I need from a relationship. Some of these needs are not negotiable, yet others are important and there are others still which I would class as 'nice to have'.

I believe you can't go too far wrong if you know what they are.

For example, in my case, top of the list of my non-negotiables is that my new partner would have to be kind. This is something you can tell from the very beginning of meeting somebody new, not just from how they treat you but also by observing how they treat and talk to and about other people.

Another of my non-negotiable needs is to be listened to as well as to have the opportunity to listen to others. This means a future partner would have to be willing to open up and to share his experiences with me; otherwise, there'd be nothing for me to listen to!

Tenderness is also a non-negotiable. Without it, I think I'd starve emotionally!

I went on to identify other really important needs (one level down from the non-negotiables):

I think it is important for him to have one or more interests that keep him engaged because it keeps him interesting. We would then always have things to talk about and he wouldn't be possessive and needy for my constant company.

I also want him to have his own mates or at least one important mate. I firmly believe that friends are essential, not just for us women but for men as well. It gives them an additional outlet for socialising with other men.

And, most importantly, I wanted him to be close to his family because I think it says a lot about a man but, of course, there are exceptions, if his family is dysfunctional, for example.

All of these things are easily identifiable from the very beginning of a new relationship - by the way he talks about himself, his past experiences in relationships, about his friendships, about his interests, his family, and so on.

By the way, watch out if he's reluctant to talk about his past.

This is how the first two or three meetings with Paul went.

As I tend to do when I meet someone new, I asked questions. That's not only because I'm genuinely interested but also because, from past experience, I believe that men like to talk about themselves.

Then, after a while of answering my questions, he told me he wanted to know about me too which, again from past experience, was a bit of a novelty for me.

I soon noticed that he not only listened, but also thought afterwards about what I'd said and, sometimes, he would bring it up next time we met up. In my experience, that was pretty awesome!

Over the next couple of meetings, I learned more about his family, his sons, the lengths he went to in order to stay close to them after his divorce when they were little; about the charity he's involved in, the things he enjoys in life, about his friendships and so on.

The more I learned about him, the more I grew to like and respect him.

That, I firmly believe, makes a strong foundation for both solid friendships and love relationships.

Obviously, there's no way of knowing which way a relationship will develop – it may become a deep friendship or it may turn into love and both outcomes are to be treasured.

The point is that, without this foundation of deep liking for each other, the chances of the relationship staying strong and long-lasting are remote.

As my relationship with Paul continues to deepen and expand, I keep trying to figure out why that should be. I came to the conclusion that the secret of our ever-deepening relationship lies in our mutual compatibility.

Everybody knows how important it is to have things in common but being compatible takes this to an entirely new level.

I recently came across a book called *Getting Together and Staying Together* by William Glasser, M.D., a world-renowned psychiatrist, which he co-wrote with his wife and colleague, Carleen Glasser.

This book added a new dimension to my understanding of what it takes to build strong and loving relationships.

William and Carleen Glasser describe 5 fundamental needs:

- for survival
- for love and belonging
- for freedom
- for power
- for fun.

Their premise is that, if the strength of some of these basic needs differs significantly between you and the person you're interested in, chances are you're heading for turbulent times.

Here's an example.

Say one of you has a high need for love and belonging and the other, a need for freedom. The one with the high need for freedom might turn out to be a commitment-phobe or want to be out with his mates or her girlfriends more than with you.

You'd wonder if they are as interested in you as they say they are. Remember, actions speak louder than words.

If you pushed them to spend more time with you, they'd feel hemmed in and likely to withdraw even more, either physically or emotionally.

On the other hand, if the strength of these two needs is less extreme, there's more likely to be room for adjustment.

Here's another example.

Say one of you has a high need for power – as in more controlling or the need to be right at all costs, as I used to be. Then, if both of you have a high need for power, you will be locked in a constant power struggle.

In another example, if one of you always want to have your own way and the other feels that they always have to give in, chances are the latter will end up feeling resentful and their needs ignored.

But controlling power is only one side of the coin. The other side is the power to achieve, to make things happen, to make a difference – for which we then want to be valued and appreciated.

So, if one of you has a deep need to make a difference, chances are, it will take quite a bit of time away from being together. If you don't have a passion of your own, you may come to resent your partner for spending so much time away from you.

If, however, both of you have something that engages you beyond your own joint lives, then you will have lots to talk about when you're together. And, if you're both interested in each other's passion, then that will only serve to strengthen your bond.

How to figure out the strength of your own needs

This is an important exercise to improve your awareness. Start by thinking about the things you used to talk about with your friends as a young woman, particularly when, inevitably, you were talking about boys.

As a young woman, did you complain that this boy was always trying to get you into bed while what you wanted was for him to tell you he loved you? Did you mention a boy who was always off with his mates and had limited time for you? And what about the commitment-phobic – that's evidence of a very high need for freedom.

And what about you? Do you tend to feel attracted to people who are emotionally and practically unavailable – as in married?

These ideas are particularly helpful, first because they enable you to figure out the strength of your own fundamental needs and, second, because you can then compare them with someone you have only just met for whom you feel a strong attraction.

I urge you to think about them before you rush into a serious relationship.

And so, back to Paul and me. This is what I finally understood.

- Paul and I both have a high need for *love and belonging* – not just towards each other but, in his case, to his family, his sons, his mates and now, me. In my case, my friends are just as important to me – and now, there's Paul.

- Paul and I share a similar strength of need for *freedom*. We're a 'living apart together' couple which means that we both have our own life, one that is meaningful to us and that we focus on during the week. Then, on weekends, our strong need for *love and belonging* for each other kicks in.

- Paul and I both have a very low need for (controlling) *power* which makes it very easy to be together, without feeling defensive or wanting to make it clear that one of us is right and the other wrong (as I did with Jim). At the same time, we both have a very high need for *power* to achieve something of value, to make a difference and to be acknowledged and appreciated. That fits very well with our need for time to ourselves to do the things that matter to us.

- We both have a high need for *fun,* enjoy learning new things and having a good laugh. That makes our time together really enjoyable.

The No. 1 need, the need for *survival* which revolves around finances – a preference for saving versus spending (an important source of strife in a relationship), does not apply to us because we don't live together.

In Chapter 9, under Secret No. 6, about the importance of good communications, I have again quoted the same fundamental needs but in a different context.

But reasonably compatible need strengths are not the only indicators of what makes you feel happy in your relationship.

The other is how you feel when you are with this person.

When I was with Jim I felt unloved and unimportant. I felt I didn't matter to him.

In contrast, when I'm with Paul I feel loved, beautiful, sexy, interesting, safe, accepted – and more. And I know, because he told me, he feels special, wanted, accepted and safe so he knows he can tell me anything, however personal and I won't judge him.

How do you feel when you're with your partner?

Secret No. 4 – To change another person's behaviour you need to change the way you engage with them

> *"I learned a long time ago that no one can change another person's behaviour but we can give them the tools, resources and understanding to change their own behaviour."*
> *Chet Bialicki, Teen Leadership Coordinator, Westbrook High School, Westbrook, Maine, USA.*

Changing another person's behaviour starts with whether or not you believe yourself to be worthy of being treated with kindness, thoughtfulness and yes, with respect.

It is our self-perception that, subconsciously, teaches people how to treat us – they take us at our own valuation.

If we don't like ourselves, why should they? If we take ourselves for granted, why shouldn't they take us for granted too? If we keep putting ourselves down, why wouldn't they believe it's OK to treat us carelessly too? If we tolerate unacceptable behaviour, why shouldn't they continue to treat us that way? If we don't think we're likeable, lovable, attractive, why should anybody else?

In Chapter 7, under Secret No. 1: 'To change your life you need to become self-aware', I invited you to start noticing what you do that works for you and what you do that doesn't work so well. Also, notice the things that happen and how they make you feel.

In the context of changing the way people treat you, you need to figure out your personal boundaries. Personal boundaries are like a line drawn in sand – this far and no further.

The problem is that other people tend to cross your line all the time and we rarely do anything to put a stop to it.

Personal boundaries though, are critical to healthy and happy relationships. That's partly because people need to know where they stand with you and partly because having stood up for yourself, you made it clear what you regard as acceptable and what you regard as not acceptable. That will make you feel good about yourself.

But, if you have never given any thought to the question of personal boundaries, where do you start?

Here's where your feelings come in.

Reflect: what behaviours upset you, make you feel angry, hurt, resentful?

Notice how you respond. Do you sulk? Do you go on the counter-attack? Do you become sarcastic or give that person the cold shoulder?

If that's how you deal with unacceptable behaviour or behaviour that makes you feel uncomfortable ask yourself, does it change anything?

If it doesn't make any difference to a difficult situation, does it make you feel fed up?

If so, now is the time to change things.

Exercise 1

Make a list of at least 10 frequently experienced, unacceptable situations which you would like to change.

For example, do you spend time with people who are generally critical or negative? Do you feel drained when you're with them? Can you think of somebody where, after spending time with them, you end up feeling bad about yourself because they're critical and negative about you and others?

Now think back to this kind of situation. If you would like things to be different, what changes could you make?

You might decide to spend less time with them and do something positive and enjoyable instead.

That would, of course, be the simplest solution but, if you can't avoid the person for whatever reason, try a different approach, for example, when they keep talking about negative things, you might say that that is not your experience.

I had a friend who kept talking about how rude, careless, thoughtless and generally incompetent people were.

I remember replying, "How strange, because that's not my experience at all!" She seemed surprised but didn't pursue it.

I realised I had two choices.

I could decide not to allow her attitude to drag me down and/or to see less of her.

I tried the first option and, over time, our relationship fizzled out.

Exercise 2

When people treat you unkindly and without consideration, write down as specifically as possible how you do NOT want to be treated.

Exercise 3

Now list at least 10 ways you would prefer to be treated instead.

Think of what you need and want in a relationship for you to feel happy and fulfilled – either with a friend or with your partner. If your needs and wants are not being met or, at least, not the ones that really matter to you, write those down.

Ask yourself, how do I want to feel in my relationship? Be specific, for example, if you put on your list 'I need to feel supported', add what exactly would make you feel supported.

You might include things like:

- To be listened to when I need to talk about a particular problem without them trying to solve it, unless I specifically ask for it.
- To consult me before making a decision that affects me, unless it's really minor.

See what else you come up with. Record a minimum of 10 things in every area of your life with your partner or a close friend.

Exercise 4

Write down as many situations as possible that make you feel uncomfortable in every area of your life.

Exercise 5

Reflect – what can you do to avoid or remove yourself from those situations?

Exercise 6

Think about the kind of people you would like to have in your life. List their qualities and what difference these qualities would make to you.

By the way, please don't attempt to do these exercises in one go. Space them out. Take time over each one. Record your answers in your journal.

Exercise 7

Go back to the list you made about how you do NOT want to be treated.

This list represents your personal boundaries. Divide this list into 3 sub-lists each of which represents a level.

Level 1: Behaviours that irritate you, but which you can live with without feeling resentful – this is key.

Level 2: Behaviours that matter enough to discuss with the other person.

Level 3: These are the non-negotiables, the unacceptables, where an important need is not being met. You yourself will know which they are because the fact that they are ignored means you are suffering. In addition to the non-negotiables also include behaviours in level 2 where nothing changes despite your best efforts.

In this case, there will come a point when you have to acknowledge that your partner doesn't care about you, your feelings or your relationship.

How to change unacceptable behaviour

Before you try to change unacceptable behaviour, consider first the following.

You need to accept, however hard you may find it, that people only change when they're willing and able to do so. That means that they will only change:

- if they see how important it is to you and they care enough to make the effort.
- if they see that they might benefit too. For example, they have also been unhappy and they can see there's a possibility for things to improve.

Step 1

Choose a level 2 issue (see exercise 7 above).

Ask yourself, "What exactly is missing?", "What do I want to achieve?"

Earlier on you figured out your personal boundaries.

It is really important for you to affirm them because if you allow people, whoever they may be, to get away with unacceptable behaviour, either they will believe that you don't mind being treated like that or they don't care whether you mind or not.

That would then become a level 3 issue.

A note of warning: you need to be very clear about what you want and need because this is such an important part of the change process. If you're inconsistent and send mixed messages, your partner will not take you seriously, so don't blame them if their behaviour doesn't change.

The one thing you must NOT do is to trivialise the problem, as I did for so long, for example, "Oh, well, it doesn't really matter", "It's not so bad", "I'm making a mountain out of a molehill", and so on. That's your Gremlin at work.

What does NOT work

When trying to change a person's behaviour, it helps to remember that the following does NOT work: direct accusations usually expressed in the 'you' form, as in "You're always late!", "You never do anything around the house!", "You're such a moron!" and other unhelpful ways of communicating.

There are several reasons why this approach doesn't work.

- It's aggressive. You will only provoke your partner into becoming defensive and they will either withdraw or go into counter-aggression mode, so not only will you end up fighting, but either nothing will change or things will get worse.

- The reality is that they may come back late sometimes but not 'always'. They may not do much around the house but not 'never'. And they may 'sometimes' behave like a moron (or a shrew), but not 'always'.

This way of engaging is called 'arguable' because it may or may not be true.

What is more likely to work

A more positive approach which is more likely to work, is the 'inarguable' approach, where you say something they can't dispute such as "I feel …"

The idea is to encourage a change, especially since you cannot force it. To remind you:

> *You cannot change a person's behaviour unless they're willing and able to change it.*

Something else you may want to bear in mind is that it's difficult to change habits. This is just as true for you as it is for them. That means that you will need to be *patient* and *persistent*.

You also need to be *consistent*, by which I mean not blow hot and cold, sometimes let it pass and, at other times, come down on them like a ton of bricks or start nagging them.

There are two ways to hold a conversation:

- Where you take the initiative because you feel unhappy.
- Where you both agree in advance to have a conversation about something you clash about.

There is a technique developed by William Glasser, M.D. called the problem solving circle.

The premise is that there are three entities in your relationship:

- you
- your partner
- the relationship itself.

Together, you draw an imaginary circle inside of which you're willing to negotiate the issue on which you disagree. Within this circle you're both willing to give something – with the emphasis on the word 'give'.

If you both care about the relationship, you will both be willing to enter the circle knowing that you will need to give something for the greater good of the relationship.

However, if the need is only yours then you need a different approach.

When they're feeling frustrated, people tend to exclaim, "I told them a thousand times!"

Saying the same thing again and again, the same way only slower and louder, will produce the same results – at best, no change and, at worst, resentment and frustration.

The only way to start the change process is by engaging with them in a different way. This is really important so I will repeat it:

> *The only way to get a person to change is by engaging with them in a different way.*

That 'different way' is to 'educate' them. Educating somebody is helping them to learn to do something differently. It requires, as I mentioned above, patience, persistence and consistency.

It's how you teach small children.

Preparation

First, ask yourself, "Do I really believe that I'm worth being treated with consideration?" "How important is it for me that they (the person you plan to have a conversation with) behave differently?"

Once you're clear about that, there are some important things you need to think about first.

Simply put, you need to figure out what approach works best with that person and what approach gets their back up.

What. When couples have a fight many, often women, have the habit of throwing everything at their partner, including the proverbial kitchen sink. That will only get you into a fight and won't resolve anything.

So just stop and think, what's the specific issue you want to address that's causing you distress? What exactly do you want to say? Focus on how this particular issue makes you feel.

Ask yourself, "What outcome do I want?"

Also, remember that, after the conversation, you will, at least for the time being, still be living together.

When. Choose a time when, ideally, neither of you is busy, worried or stressed.

How. It might be an idea to flag up the conversation along the lines, "There's something I would like to talk with you about. Would now be a good time or would you prefer tomorrow afternoon?" Make sure the tone alerts them if this is going to be a heavy session.

If they ask what exactly you want to talk to them about, tell them you're feeling upset or anxious about something that you want to resolve. I also suggest you add that if they have something they'd like to bring up, then that would be OK.

Where. Somewhere private.

Process. Allow enough time.

Don't forget, if you have an issue, your partner may have one too. If so, I suggest you give them the floor first. For some people it's often easier for them to listen when they've been given a chance to be heard first.

Make a decision to really listen to what they have to say. Keep encouraging them to say what's bothering them and make it clear that you are paying attention by using positive body language, nodding, saying 'aha, yes, I see'.

Whatever you do, make sure you don't jump in trying to defend your position. That would invalidate the purpose of this exercise.

How to communicate your unhappiness

Now it's your turn.

As I mentioned earlier, use 'inarguable' statements because they are most likely to get you the results you're looking for.

An inarguable statement is a two-step process:

- how something they said or did made you feel
- why it made you feel that way, that is, how you interpreted what they said or did.

This approach is called 'inarguable' because your partner cannot argue with your feelings.

Choose one specific issue that's making you feel unhappy, irritated or resentful.

Keep your words clear and unambiguous.

Step 1 – Make sure you're clear about what the issue really is

Example – you tend to go the extra mile for your partner but you feel they don't appreciate what you do for them. Plus, you feel taken for granted because you don't get much back in return.

The one thing you don't want to do is throw everything at them.

Choose the one issue that matters most to you, for example the fact that you give and give and give but feel unappreciated.

Before tackling them, stop and think. Looking back at my own marriage, this is what I noticed with the benefit of hindsight.

I, too, used to go the extra mile for Jim, as a way of showing my love for him and, perhaps like you, after a while I began to feel resentful and taken for granted because he didn't seem to notice my efforts.

Because I didn't know then what I know now, I failed to realise that not only was my giving excessive, but often I was doing things he didn't really care about.

Again, with the benefit of hindsight, I used to give and give and give because it made me feel good about myself. I saw myself as a selfless and loving person.

The big issue here is that you can't make a relationship work all by yourself. It takes two. This is why, it's so important to try and sort things out.

Step 2 — The conversation

Obviously, you need to use your own words but make sure you include things like these.

Part 1. "(This) is what I've been doing to make you feel happy. It doesn't seem to be working because I feel you don't appreciate what I do. Is there something else you would appreciate more?"

Part 2. "I would like you to …" or "What I would love you to …" - or "What would make me feel you love me would be …" – and you might add, "(this) really matters to me" (insert a need or want that you would love or need to have him meet).

Part 3. Talk about how you're feeling now, after the conversation. If they haven't had their turn yet, this is a good time to ask your partner if they're feeling resentful about something you're doing. Be sure to make it OK for them to talk to you about it.

Listen without arguing or defending (this is particularly hard).

Agree to have regular conversations so resentments don't build up.

Consequences

I used to have mixed feelings about the use of consequences because it felt manipulative and controlling.

However, work with clients has persuaded me that consequences have an important role to play.

Here are some reflections.

The consequences must cause real discomfort to have an impact, that is, it must be important enough for them to care.

Never use it as a bluffing strategy. It might explode in your face if they don't react as you hope. If that happens then you have to see it through and implement that consequence. If you don't, your credibility is damaged forever.

On the positive side, consequences can be positive or negative – like the carrot and the stick.

The idea is to make it clear how important this particular issue is to you and, hopefully, to motivate them to acknowledge your feelings and arrive at a mutually satisfactory arrangement.

Having said that, remember that you cannot force another person to change unless they're able and willing to do so.

Here are two examples.

Example 1

If the issue is that your partner keeps interrupting or shouting at you, then the consequence is that you will walk out until you can have a proper conversation.

Example 2

Here's another, more serious, example.

Eric, the 'boyfriend'/partner of a friend of mine, Lisa, had really poor driving habits. He'd drive very aggressively, cutting up other drivers and generally behaving in a 'macho' way.

Lisa would literally fear for her life and told him many times how scared his driving made her feel – all to no avail.

On this particular day, they were driving to the airport. They were on their way to their holiday destination, Malta. Lisa had been looking forward to it for the last several weeks.

Eric was, as usual, driving like a maniac (her words) and she tried, unsuccessfully, to restrain him.

Finally, she told him, "If you don't slow down, I'm not coming with you to Malta."

He didn't believe her but, as he parked the car, she got out, collected her luggage from the boot and took the bus home.

And this is the important bit.

She didn't do it because she wanted to teach him a lesson. She did it because she'd reached the end of her tether and because nothing she said made any difference.

After she had made her stand, they didn't see each other for three months but, in the end, he came back and they have been together ever since. He's made an effort to moderate his driving which is now more acceptable to her.

The point is, he cared enough about her and their relationship to make the effort – but he might not have done and she knew it.

By the way, she's 62 and he's 69 – foolhardiness is not the prerogative of the young!

What if nothing changes?

As explained above, I class an issue as level 3 in two situations.

- You've been telling them repeatedly how their behaviour makes you feel but nothing has changed. That would seem to indicate they don't care about you or your relationship. You might want to check if this is true. Ask them.

- The issue is one of the non-negotiables you identified earlier.

What if they refuse to give in or ignore you?

This is the big one.

This is where you have a choice – and it isn't an easy one.

To stay or to leave.

Staying does not necessarily mean surrender.

Having come this far in your reading, if you've done the exercises and reflections, if you've had new insights and have started seeing yourself in a different way, one that says you deserve to be treated with consideration and respect – if all these things are in place, then you will be able to make this decision – perhaps not immediately, but you will come to a point when you know what you need to do.

In my case, once I had decided I simply had to leave, it took me the better part of a year to reach the point where I felt able to tell him and then another year to put my plan into action.

That meant moving into the guest room and doing up the house for sale, because neither one of us had the money to move out until the house was sold. This I did almost single-handedly, because he wasn't motivated to help me leave.

But making the decision is the big one. This is the point of no return.

However, 'no return' doesn't mean that you have to leave the relationship nor does it mean, as I said above, that you're surrendering or giving up.

What it does mean is that you're staying for a reason that has NOTHING to do with fear of the unknown, nor fear of being on your own or fear of not being capable of seeing it through. This is all in the past.

Often one reason for staying can be that, having done all your research, you realise that it is genuinely financially impossible for you to leave, at least for the time being.

If that's the case, and you decide to stay – then do so, but let go of your resentments. Stop complaining and stop regarding yourself as a victim. You may be staying, but everything has changed and you're now staying from a position of strength. The new boundaries have been set.

This is an opportunity to build a new life for yourself, for example by no longer making your partner your priority but putting yourself first for a change.

Remember, today we live between 20 and 30 years longer than our great-grandparents did, so you may want to ask yourself how you want those years to be.

Whatever form these extra bonus years takes, it must be rewarding.

Of course, you need to tell your partner of your decision so you're transparent and authentic.

Planning the next stage of your life may require outside help. Your best bet is a coach. Ask for advice and speak with more than one before you decide with whom you feel most comfortable. A coach will work closely with you, helping you to move your life forwards towards fulfilment, happiness and wellbeing. They also help you move through the obstacles that lie ahead.

Chapter 9 – Emotional communication – The Emotional Revitaliser System

Secret No. 5 – Friendship is at the heart of every happy relationship

> *"Relationships are stronger when you're best friends first and a couple second."*
> *Arjun Loveable*

Research into what keeps couples together who have been happily married 40, 50 or even 60 years shows that it is friendship more than romantic love that bonds them.

Love takes work and that work is made possible because of that friendship.

Long-lasting relationships start with a deep friendship.

How do you know you're really friends? You know when:

- you like and respect each other
- you accept each other as you really are, without judging, so you know you can trust each other completely
- you accept and respect each other's views, opinions and feelings, even when you disagree
- you both give and take things the other values – in other words, your relationship is reciprocal
- you care for each other's wellbeing
- you encourage each other to pursue the freedom to do your own thing
- you put yourself out for each other when you know it matters, even if you don't particularly want to do it
- you value and appreciate each other and say so often
- you enjoy each other's company and have fun together.

These are some of the key ingredients that get you through life's turbulences and enable you to enjoy the good times even more when you share them with each other.

When you have this kind of friendship, you're stronger and better able to face life's storms together.

With this solid foundation of friendship when you're irritated, frustrated or resentful with each other, as you will inevitably be from time to time, especially in a long relationship, you will be willing to communicate your feelings in such a way that you can hear each other without feeling hurt or defensive.

The one thing true friends never do is try to control each other or stop them from being who they are.

Friends know that they can only change themselves. The only thing they can control is their own behaviour which includes everything they think, feel, say and do.

When you're friends, you also know that the relationship matters as much as your own needs and wants.

What if you don't feel friendly towards your long-term partner?

Intention

Assuming your relationship really matters to you, you start with an intention.

An intention comes from the heart; it comes from love.

What sometimes happens is that, even though the love is still there, it may have been buried under layers and layers of frustrations, irritations, resentments and hurts that you have accumulated over the years.

However, if your relationship truly matters to you, then you need to realise that rekindling a loving and mutually appreciative relationship takes time, patience, persistence, self-compassion, commitment and a specific set of skills.

As I mentioned under *The Authentic Self-Exploration Roadmap*, our negative feelings start in our head with a choice (yes, a choice) to hold on to our resentments.

As bizarre as it may sound, there's something seductive about holding on to our resentments, that feeling "I'm right and you're wrong". And you may well choose to be right rather than to be happy. This is definitely one of those either-or choices because, in this life, you can't always be both right and happy.

How can you overcome your resentments?

Here are some suggestions which may open the door to rekindling the love you once had for your partner.

When you think about your partner:

- remember what attracted you in the first place, focus on the things you like about them rather than on the ones you find irritating

- deliberately look for things to appreciate and compliment them often instead of judging and criticising,

- acknowledge all positive efforts (the ones you stopped noticing) instead of taking them for granted
- be clear about your partner's needs and wants
- imagine what it might feel like to be at the receiving end of your dissatisfaction
- imagine life without your partner.

To sum up

Your intention is the 'why', and the tools I'm sharing with you in this book are the 'how'.

Without a 'why' it's far too easy to become discouraged when things don't go as you expect or when it takes longer than you imagined it would, as is bound to happen sometimes.

When you find it's harder than you thought it would be, that's when you're most likely to come up with all kinds of excuses, justifications and defensiveness which, for some strange reason, sound valid and reasonable.

Your intention is the one thing that keeps bringing you back on track and makes it all worth it.

How to set your intention

When it comes to setting intentions toward your goals, there are 5 essential steps.

Let go of limiting beliefs and change your mindset

(Chapter 7, Secret 1: 'To change your life you need to become self-aware'.) Limiting beliefs are driven by the Gremlin, our negative inner critic. They are the ones that hinder or slow us down, especially when we decide to make positive changes that take us out of our comfort zone and directly challenge our Gremlin.

In this context, limiting beliefs may fall into the following areas.

- That you don't deserve (this good thing).

- That (this) is never going to work – because you're just not good enough, strong enough, wise enough and, anyway, it's too late.

- That (this) is never going to work – because the other person is a moron, pig-headed and just plain selfish. Plus, they don't care anyway. This makes it easy to feel justified in blaming them if it doesn't work.

Be clear, but flexible

Be clear in your mind what intention you want to set, for example, "I want to be close to Nick (or Jane) again. I want us to respect each other, and be loving and supportive" "I want my friendship with Janet to be caring and honest again."

Bring in all your senses

Write it all down describing your intention using all your senses. Imagine what it will feel like, what it will look like, what it will sound like when you have achieved your intention; how your life together will be different.

Take action

To achieve the changes you intend, you need to use the tools you're learning in this book. The best way to make changes without becoming overwhelmed is by taking small steps.

There's a saying that goes like this:

"How do you eat an elephant? In small bite sizes."

In other words, take baby steps. But, even though they're small, they still need to be taken if you want to bring about the changes you say you want!

Keep yourself on track

Remind yourself of your intentions by writing them down in your journal and looking at them every day. This is a great way to keep reminding yourself – again and again – why you're doing what you're doing.

Also, record the actions you've chosen to take and how they worked.

When you do this, it will not only show your progress, lack of it and why that might be (keep track of your Gremlin) but it will also strengthen your confidence.

Remember:

- this is an ongoing journey
- results may take time to show.

Secret No. 6 – Good communication is central to every happy relationship

> *"Assumptions and lack of communication are the number one relationship killers. We all perceive things differently. We've lived different lives, we have different views. Understand that before getting angry at someone for not believing what you believe."*
>
> *Anon.*

As I was growing up, my parents drummed it into me how important it was for people to like me. They explained that my very survival depended on it.

It sounds a bit drastic, I know, but it makes sense when you realise that, just before the Nazis invaded Prague, it was people's goodwill that got them out to safety – although you might reasonably say that circumstances were different when I was growing up.

It will, therefore, not come as a surprise to you when I tell you that I became absolutely terrified of conflict. Jim was equally put off by conflict so, what do you do with the anger, resentments and frustrations that swirl around in your body?

One option (my preferred one in those days) was to nag over and over again and, when that didn't work, I'd have a temper tantrum. In response, Jim would simply walk away, leaving me standing there, fuming.

OK, so this option didn't work.

There are two important things I have learned over the years.

- You cannot force anybody to do anything they don't want to do. When you try, as I did, they either push back or withdraw. It only causes resentment and frustration.

- Your differences and the things you fight about are not because they're pig-headed and unwilling to recognise that you're right but rather because you are two people with different needs which are not being met.

So, to state the obvious, I was communicating really badly but, even if I'd known about our differing needs not being met, I wouldn't have been able to do anything about it.

Why?

Because the foundation wasn't in place – I didn't know or like myself, I didn't know or like Jim, I didn't trust either one of us and I certainly didn't feel emotionally safe with him.

That's what this work is all about.

But, assuming you're well on your way to building a solid friendship, here's what you might like to communicate over a period of time.

- When something happens that makes you feel sad or disappointed, when you feel unsettled, unsure of yourself, when something great happens you can't wait to share it with them, in other words, the good, the bad and the ugly.
- Tell them that you love them.
- Say "I'm sorry" when you're clearly in the wrong or even when you suspect you might have been wrong or thoughtless or careless or forgot something that you knew mattered to your partner.

But here's the clincher.

Your actions are the other branch of communication so remember:

Actions and words are equally important.

It's both the words and the behaviours combined that make the difference.

To know what actions would be most valued by your partner find out what matters to them, what their needs and wants really are – rather than assuming you know.

Plus, it's how you consistently treat them over the long term until it becomes a habit that will enable them to know whether you really love them or whether you're just going through the motions.

As I have mentioned repeatedly, if you want to make changes in your relationship then you will have to take the first step.

As we know, life happens. Something happens that makes you feel angry, frustrated, hurt or resentful. Here's where you will be tested.

First, don't assume they meant to hurt or upset you. At the same time, if something did hurt or upset you, you need to deal with it. A safe assumption is that there's something that upset them too or they wouldn't have said or done what they did, so blaming or going on the attack are strategies that will undo all the good work you've done so far.

To remind you, your relationship is composed of three separate entities:

- you
- your partner
- your relationship.

If your relationship truly matters to you, you may have to be the one who offers a concession first.

Entrenched positions don't help get you what you want and, since you can only control your own behaviour and not anybody else's, it's up to you.

Before you start the conversation, it might be worth revisiting your needs and wants but this time do something else:

Think about what, in the light of your knowledge of your partner, you think their needs and wants might be.

Courtesy of William Glasser, M.D., who I quoted in the section about finding the right partner for you, there are five significant needs you both share but, perhaps in different strengths which is why you're having problems getting along.

In the context of your existing relationship, these needs are for:

- **Survival** – which includes money – saving it, spending it. If there are differences here then one might accuse the other of being either mean or irresponsible.

- **Love and belonging** – if, for example, one wants more closeness and the other more freedom then it could explain why one or the other feels unloved.

- **Freedom** – when one wants to spend time away from the relationship, for example go to the pub with his mates or going shopping with your girlfriends. If your partner has a need for freedom that's stronger than yours while you have a need for love and belonging that is stronger than theirs – there will be pain, frustration and resentment – plus, sometimes, accusations of being clingy or selfish.

- **Power** – a need to control and manipulate to get one's own way. Some people have a strong need for control but, if their partner doesn't really mind then it won't be a problem. The problem arises if both need to control the other and you get into a power struggle.

- There's another need for power which I explained earlier: the power to make a difference. So if one of you has a passion that takes a lot of their time, unless you have one of your own, it will certainly be a bone of contention.

- **Fun** – which includes enjoyment, pleasure, learning new things together or separately.

Therefore, if your relationship is suffering then the reason might be that:

- you differ in the strength of a particular need, for example your need for freedom is high and your partner's is low. Or, conversely, your need for love and belonging is high and your partner's is low.

- those needs conflict with each other, for example, the need for love and belonging conflicts with the need for freedom. So, blaming your partner for having a need that's not as strong as yours is unreasonable and won't get you anywhere because he will be unable to change.

When you understand both your needs and theirs, then you will be better able to approach the problem you're wrestling with – a need that's not being met – in a more positive and productive way.

So, given the above, think about what you're willing to do to help the relationship. I'm thinking concession, not surrender, because your needs will also have to be taken into account.

People tend to deal with their differences in two ways:

- conflict
- disagreement.

Conflict

Conflict doesn't work because it doesn't solve anything.

When you're in conflict, chances are you're not talking to each other or, if you are, then only coldly.

One of you might say in an aggrieved tone of voice, "What did I do now?" and the other might reply, feeling equally aggrieved "You know very well what you did! And it's not the first time either!" – which gets neither one of you anywhere.

Usually, both of you tend to assume the other one has a malicious intent to the point when you cannot even hear each other.

In the worst-case scenario, if feelings run really high, you might scream at, and over, each other. Or there may be so much accumulated resentment that you might even throw everything at them, stuff going back years.

Neither one of you really talks or listens.

The issues are not discussed and misunderstandings are not clarified which means they cannot be resolved.

Disagreements

Disagreements are completely different. Even big ones, are unlikely to degenerate into conflict probably because there's a foundation of liking and respect in your relationship.

This is hugely important because, even if you're in a middle of a disagreement, you're less likely to run roughshod over your partner, you're less likely to try to manipulate, control, go on the counter-attack or fight dirty.

You don't assume a malicious intent. You try to check first if there's a misunderstanding, for example, whether a particular word has the same meaning for both of you.

My partner, Paul, and I have been in situations where the intention could not have been more different from the one (he or I) first assumed. I've now learned to double-check.

When you disagree, you usually know what it's about. You talk to each other about it and you both know where the other stands on this particular issue.

Most importantly, you can both talk to each other afterwards without having chipped away at the liking, love and respect you have for each other.

You will at least understand why your partner thinks and feels as they do even if you don't agree.

If the disagreement affects your relationship then you're much more likely to talk it through, listen, negotiate and, if necessary, reach a compromise.

However, reaching a compromise that works for both of you is entirely different from compromising yourself. You compromise yourself when you give in without getting something you value in return.

This would only cause lingering resentment which is more likely to happen in a conflict situation.

The main difference between conflict and disagreements is that conflict is about the person, while disagreements are about the issues.

Here's the bottom line.

Expressing any hurts or anger in such a way that your partner can hear you without feeling defensive or judged, is a communication skill that is absolutely critical to maintain the love and respect for each other in the long term.

Chapter 10 – The Passion and Intimacy Generator

Secret No. 7 – Intimacy is only possible when you both feel safe

> *"An intimate relationship is one that allows you to be yourself."*
> Deepak Chopra

This is where it all comes together.

To get to those loving feelings takes dedication and, as I mentioned in the previous modules, commitment, patience and persistence.

Before we get started, I want to recap on what we have covered in the three previous modules.

We have to know and understand ourselves

We rarely truly know ourselves. Distorted, false and mixed messages which we have absorbed since childhood mean that we have lost touch with who we really are. I don't mean this in a spiritual but in a strictly practical sense.

We need to reconnect with our own needs and wants, we need to understand ourselves, what makes us tick, what's important to us, what is true for us, and, especially, what does and doesn't work for us.

We have to like ourselves

I can't emphasise this too often and it's never too late to achieve this.

Far too many of us don't really like ourselves. We are bombarded with messages all around us telling us in hundreds of different ways that we're not good enough until we end up believing it. Sometimes, we are aware of this belief but, mostly, we are not.

Because of these beliefs, most of us treat ourselves abominably. We beat ourselves up, put ourselves at the bottom of our list of priorities, pretend we're helpless and that there's nothing we can do to change our situation, and much more.

As a result, people take us at our own low valuation.

However, when we like ourselves, we're absolutely clear in our own mind how we do NOT want to be treated and also exactly how we prefer others to treat us.

This means we're also prepared to clearly ask for what we want while, at the same time, being aware that, even though we may not always get what we ask for, we will certainly get much more than if we hadn't asked at all.

Being ignored is unacceptable. End of story. That applies to friends, shop assistants and, especially, your partner.

We have to trust ourselves

Only when we know and understand ourselves can we then trust ourselves to make choices which really work for us.

By the time we reach this point of self-trust, we can then also accept it when, inevitably, our choices don't turn out the way we had hoped. With our newly-acquired self-knowledge we can handle the disappointment, the failure or the setback, learn from the experience and try again next time.

This has been the journey you embarked on with this programme.

- You either focused on transforming your existing relationship, if it doesn't make you happy, or …

- … if you're not currently in a relationship, you now have a clearer idea of the kind of person who will be right for you.

We reciprocate

This means that there's a healthy balance in the relationship, where you both give and take and where both your own and your partner's needs are met. Only then can relationships thrive.

Once these things are in place, you will be ready to take your conscious loving to the next level.

In the previous module you will have learned how to establish warm feelings through the power of friendship. Now you'll be ready to take the next steps towards building emotional intimacy.

But, as with friendship, it's up to you to take the initiative. Why?

Because life happens. You may not have tomorrow. All you have is right now. Don't waste it!

Always remember, to love and to be loved is the most precious thing there is. Don't take it for granted!

How to generate emotional intimacy

There are 5 behaviours that are both individually and collectively very powerful in enabling you to move forward towards a loving and intimate relationship.

Show your partner acceptance and compassion

Accepting your partner and being non-judgemental are absolutely fundamental.

To me, making your partner feel inadequate is the number one crime we can commit against another person, never mind the person we say we love – and the one I admit to having committed against Jim, by wanting to change him pretty much from the word go.

As I mentioned earlier, accepting your partner doesn't mean we have to agree with everything they say or do but it's important to remember that, when we disagree, it's because beliefs vary, as do our background, upbringing and all other life experiences.

If we'd had the same childhood and subsequent experiences as they did, for example, chances are we would have the same opinion and beliefs as they do. That's why we need to accept as a fact of life that we both bring different background, life experience and baggage into our relationship.

Accepting our partner requires compassion, empathy and concern as well as a desire for their wellbeing. We believe in them, even if (or when) they don't believe in themselves.

Accepting our differences in a non-judgemental, compassionate and accepting way is one of the most wonderful gifts we can give.

Here's a tip: when you find it difficult to let go of your judgements, remind yourself that you, too, are imperfect and give them some slack.

Being imperfect is what it means to be human.

Show your partner you appreciate them

Appreciation is absolutely critical to us feeling loved and accepted. If our relationship feels unfulfilling, then what's missing can often be traced to simple lack of appreciation.

Telling yourself you're too busy to make time for the all-important appreciation is just an excuse and one that will cost you dearly in the long term.

Take the time to focus on what they do or some qualities which you like or even love.

When you decide to look for the things you like about them, I guarantee you will rediscover personal qualities that attracted you early on in your relationship which you have stopped noticing. Look also for the things they do that make a positive difference in your relationship which you may be taking for granted or which are buried under the pile of negatives.

Appreciating somebody includes complimenting them, expressing affection, for example with a hug, an affectionate touch or a smile.

However you express your appreciation make sure that, whatever you appreciate, you really mean it.

Show your partner that you acknowledge them

Acknowledging somebody is different from appreciating them. When you acknowledge your partner, you show that you value them, that they matter to you.

How do you acknowledge them? Here are some ideas.

- Make them feel understood, for example, by asking questions, listening attentively to the answer and, most importantly, by remembering what they said and how they felt. If appropriate, follow up.

- Share their feelings and validate them or, in other words, make it OK for them to feel as they do, even if you don't understand.

- Show them affection with a friendly touch or a hug.

- Do random acts of kindness without being asked. Make them a cup of tea or do something else that would make them feel valued and appreciated.

- Give them space. Space gives you a breather from the intensity of life and relationships – with you and with others.

Make yourself emotionally vulnerable

This is at the heart of intimacy.

There's only one way to create a place where both of you feel safe together and, as scary as it feels, that way is to make yourself emotionally vulnerable.

Making yourself emotionally vulnerable is the one most important part in a trusting and intimate relationship.

I fully realise that making yourself emotionally vulnerable is one of the hardest things anybody can do. That's because it requires you to expose your innermost secrets, hopes, fears, doubts, pain, sadness, hurts – even your flaws, real or imagined.

Please remember that making yourself emotionally vulnerable is a gradual process. Start by sharing something that is meaningful to you and see how your partner responds then, another time, share something else.

I still remember vividly the moment when I was being coached and I knew this had to be my next step.

What I found was that, to a large extent, I could make myself emotionally vulnerable with people outside my home but, with Jim, it was virtually impossible. I did try but the look of incomprehension on his face hurt me deeply.

I then reminded myself that I was doing this for me, not for him. Making myself emotionally vulnerable was what I had to do if I wanted to become authentic. And, most of all, I needed to make myself emotionally vulnerable if I wanted to attract authentic people into my life.

However, this shouldn't be as hard for you as it was for me. At the time I hadn't yet laid the foundation necessary for this step to work.

My self-confidence and my sense of self were still fragile and I hadn't done any of the preliminary steps such as making it clear how I wanted him to treat me, know my true needs and wants and ask for them to be met – or meet some of them myself.

More important still, I hadn't done what was needed to initiate the process of building a friendship between us.

The jump to making myself emotionally vulnerable to him was a jump too far and too high.

Why is emotional vulnerability so important to an intimate relationship?

Emotional vulnerability is important because:

- it enables you to express who you really are – after years of hiding behind many different masks, trying to be acceptable and accepted
- it helps you become close and connected to your partner
- it builds trust

- it opens your heart so it's even easier to give and receive love

- making yourself emotionally vulnerable requires you to expand your comfort zone. You will find it easier to listen to your partner without becoming defensive

- when you open yourself up, you will discover it also affects your social life and increases the potential for making friendships that are warm, open-hearted and supportive.

You will be amazed to find that, when you make yourself emotionally vulnerable, you begin to reconnect with stuff you had kept hidden deep within yourself because it hurt too much.

- When you reconnect with it, when you stop running away from it or hiding from it, you will allow feelings to surface, the ones you pretended didn't exist or that you tried to ignore.

- When these feelings surface from this dark place within you and are exposed to the light, you heal the pain you kept hidden.

- When you make yourself emotionally vulnerable, you connect with your own humanity, which allows others to make themselves emotionally vulnerable to you too. This is another way to open your heart to love.

- Making yourself emotionally vulnerable makes you more attractive because people are attracted to people who are authentic. People tend to feel inhibited in the face of perfection; they tend to feel inhibited with those who appear to be always in control and come across as too independent. That's because people need to be needed; otherwise, what's the point of the relationship?

The opposite of independence isn't dependence: it's interdependence.

Develop a new habit

Develop the habit of regularly discussing with your partner what you like or love about them and what's good about your relationship. Here too you need to take the initiative.

How to generate passion

First, I have to make it clear I'm not a sex therapist and, for some of you, seeing one may be a positive step to take – either on your own or as a couple.

The first obvious point to make is that every couple and every individual within that couple is different – different needs, different personalities, different histories.

Moreover, different stages of your life will have different demands on your time.

When you're younger, there may be children or ageing parents to consider while ageing may bring problems related to health, self-confidence and self-esteem.

Needs and wants too change over time.

In the early days of my marriage I longed for Jim to tell me "I love you" and for him to, occasionally, bring me flowers, neither of which he ever did.

Over the years my needs changed to needing to be listened to and given practical support. I had a full-time job and he hadn't worked for many years – first due to redundancy and then when he became officially retired.

The fact that those needs were not met was a source of deep sadness and resentment.

As for love-making, I continued to approach him because I still longed for closeness and tenderness. The fact that I never experienced either yet kept trying still fills me with incomprehension.

What can go wrong?

There may be an accumulation of unresolved resentments that seep into the bedroom.

There are many things that can damage a relationship and which can cause sexual interest in each other to diminish. Over time, when love-making stops, it can create distance with neither one of you being aware what actually caused it.

It may be you've been together for so long that love-making has gradually become less important – for one or both of you. Or, when you do have sex, it may be so boring as to make you wonder why you even bothered.

Needs, including sexual needs, not only change over time but yours and your partner's may also differ.

Or it could be the demands of everyday life have left one or both of you too exhausted to bother.

Or your self-confidence lessens as you age and you regard yourself as physically less attractive.

If neither one of you minds that your love life has taken a back seat then that might be alright although, if not rekindled at some point, your whole relationship will suffer because sex is an important part of a loving relationship.

How to rekindle your love life

As I've been inviting you all along, you need to start with yourself. Work through these exercises and record the results in your journal.

Exercise 1

Look at yourself in the mirror.

When you're at home with your partner, do you make an effort with your appearance or have you stopped bothering?

Exercise 2

When you look at your partner, do they still make an effort or have they stopped bothering too?

Exercise 3

You have already figured out what you need to feel loved outside the bedroom. Now take the next step.

Ask yourself, what do you need to feel loved and seen as a woman – or as a man – in the bedroom?

You notice that your partner has let themselves go and your feelings of attraction towards them has diminished. Even so, it would be better to start with your own appearance.

Not only will it make your partner sit up and take notice but it will do wonders for your own self-confidence.

Record some of the things you could do to make a start.

Elsewhere I have mentioned tenderness, cuddles and other expressions of affection. These things make both of you feel seen and appreciated and that goes a long way towards improving your love life.

The next step is to introduce romance. Believe it or not, you have already started if:

- you're showing them you value and appreciate them

- you're showing a genuine interest in them by really listening to them
- you carry out random acts of kindness
- you tell them you love them, bring them little gifts, touch them tenderly, show them how much they matter to you and/or you do something for them to ease some of their everyday burden
- you have started making yourself emotionally vulnerable. As I mentioned, this can be a huge challenge for many people so it's a good idea to take it slowly.

Below are more ideas about introducing romance into your relationship.

In this context, if you have begun to feel insecure about your appearance, this can get in the way of your sex life.

Making the most of your appearance is a good start but it may not be enough.

When I met Paul, after a while I started thinking about making love with him. I hadn't had sex not only in the 12 years I'd lived on my own but for years while I was still married. Even then, the experience wasn't exactly earth-shattering.

Also, as I have scoliosis, my body is a bit off-centre. And then there is the law of gravity and other physical changes that come with age.

None of those things ever worried me while I was convinced nobody would ever see me naked. Enter Paul and I really started worrying.

But this is what actually happened.

At every stage he made it clear he saw me as a beautiful woman. At this point I had choices – to tell myself he was either blind or mad, or to believe him.

I chose to believe him.

What also made a difference was that I feel safe with him.

All of these things are powerful ways of making your partner feel loved, and when people feel loved it can translate into a desire for love-making.

And there's more you can do to introduce romance. Romance puts a twinkle in your eye.

As with most things, what is romantic varies from person to person and from couple to couple.

- For Paul and me it's going on what we call 'micro-adventures'. These are planned outings. Sometimes we do things we've done before which we both enjoyed and, at other times, we like to try out something new. If you're new to each other as we are, one of you may suggest something you think the other might also find interesting and/or enjoyable. Some outings are planned while others are spontaneous.

- We have interesting conversations. It's a great way of discovering more about each other. If you've been together a number of years you might delude yourself into believing you know everything there is to know about your partner. You couldn't be more wrong! Ask yourself, does your partner know everything there is to know about you?

- Best of all, Paul and I enjoy a good laugh together.

Now it's your turn.

Exercise 4

What is your idea of romance?

What do you think is your partner's idea of romance?

Now check with your partner. Do your ideas about what he regards as romantic match the reality?

These exercises and reflections and all the others in this book facilitate the ebb and flow of the emotional give and take in a strong and loving relationship. They enable you to recognise and meet your own and your partner's intimate needs which will leave you both with a feeling of love, closeness and intimacy.

In conclusion

Having read this book, I hope you've taken the time to reflect about how you chose your partner. Would you choose differently if you were in a position to do so?

Also, have you figured out what wounded your relationships – current or past? What can you learn from the experience?

Happy relationships are a gift – don't take them for granted and, above all, don't waste them!

> *"You cannot predict the future. You both need to give your all to the relationship you're in. You both need to do your best to care for each other. You both need to communicate authentically with each other. And you both need to give each other the last drop of love you have."*
> Sue Plumtree

Please feel free to write a review of this book and post it on Amazon.

Do connect with me on my website, sueplumtree.com, or on Facebook.

I am available for interview and can be contacted via my website.

Last words ...

I wrote this book because, having been in a relationship with a man who was reserved and distant, a man with no empathy and poor communication skills and then having found the deepest and truest love in 2015 aged 70, I made it my mission to share with you everything I learned so you too can experience love and intimacy.

This book will continue to support you every time you feel stuck and in need of a nudge or reminder.

Also, I'm only an email away – sue@sueplumtree.com.

My very best wishes for a loving and fulfilling relationship. You deserve nothing less!

Much love,

Sue Plumtree
The Over 50s Love Specialist

Special offer

Thank you for reading my book.

Here are two special offers, just for you. To take them up, contact me via sueplumtree.com and let me know you saw them in this book.

One hour coaching session

Normally £200 – for just £50.

Just let me know what you would like to talk about.

My 6-month programme

10% off my programme *Live Your Best Years Yet*.

In this six-month coaching programme we'll work together intensively to transform your experience of close relationships and make the journey towards greater happiness and fulfilment.

Live Your Best Years Yet is based on my system *The Ultimate Conscious Loving Formula* on which this book is based.

Acknowledgements

In a strange way, I have Jim to thank for this book. Had I not experienced all the pain in my first marriage, I would not have been able to learn from the experience and write it.

Also, without Paul to whom I dedicate this book, I would not have learned what it takes to build a relationship that is loving, strong and intimate.

I'm deeply grateful to Ruth Durbin who, in her role of ACE Mentor at the Professional Speakers Academy, mentored me so I was able to develop my Unique Branding System: 'The Ultimate Conscious Loving Formula'. This system became the structure of my book and made it possible for me to offer my ideas in a new and easy to follow way.

My heartfelt thanks to readers who have taken the trouble to read my manuscript and give me feedback, and especially to those who took the time to make specific suggestions that have enriched this book.

Ajayi Oguntokun

Bernadette Tonge

Joan Mercer

Leslie Calland

Marva Johnson-Jones

Mona De Silva

Phil Matthews

Zoe Meyer for loving and patient editing. Thanks to her, this book is all I hoped it would be.

Tim Gray for designing the front cover and for layout and formatting.

Thea Backhouse for proofreading my manuscript.